D1684977

THE SECRET IRON OF THE HEART

THE SECRET IRON
OF THE HEART

SONGS

AT THE FORGE OF AWAKENING MAN

Collected Poems

by

ARVIA MACKAYE EGE

ADONIS PRESS
Hawthorne Valley / Ghent, New York

CONTENTS

To
my husband
KARL EGE

CONTRIBUTORS
TO THE PUBLICATION OF THIS VOLUME

For their help with the preparation and final ap-
pearance of this volume, the author wishes to express
special, heartfelt gratitude to:

Christy Barnes, comrade upon the path of poetry, for
her share in it both as lifelong fellow-poet and now as
publishing editor —

To Margaret and George de Ris, for years of encouragement and of inner caring for its contents, and for their
generous part in bringing it to book-form, whereby the
dedication of their lives to the creation and renewal of
the arts accompanies this book wherever it goes —

And particularly, both for their concern and their
generous aid, to Thea Stanley Hughes, who has previously
published a few of these poems, to Charlotte Parker,
Theodora Richards, Joan Pyle Dufault and Agnes Mac-
beth; also, for all her skilled proof-reading, to Sandra
Sherman; and to Christopher and Diane Bamford for their
helpful book-maker's advice.

Give me not smooth, gleaming words
    That glisten from the brain,
Nor those which soar upon utopian wings,

But simple, heart-hewn words —
    Words with straight, clear eyes
Which, viewing evil, vow to heal all things;

Words that walk with sturdy feet
    As living will-warm beings
To serve the depth and dignity of man;

Or, pausing with unhurried breath,
    Hark, to harvest clear
The music of the mysteries they scan,

When, waking out of barren dream
    Within the brittle mind,
They drink the well-springs of all uttered life,

And, as free sun-begotten creatures,
    Pour the cleansing freshets
Of their song upon our mortal strife.

Prelude:

DOORWAY TO DESTINY

*Poems Written
in Childhood and Adolescence*

"The Hermit Thrush" was originally published in the Prologue to *Sanctuary — A Bird Masque*, by Percy MacKaye, and was set to music by the composer, Frederick Converse. It also appeared in *Braithwait's Anthology*; and a number of these childhood poems were published at that time in the *Little Review*, *The Outlook* and other periodicals.

THE HERMIT THRUSH

While walking through a lonely wood
    I heard a lovely voice;
A voice so fresh and true and good
    It made my heart rejoice.

It sounded like a Sunday bell
    Rung softly in a town,
Or like a stream, that in a dell
    Forever trickles down.

It seemed to be a voice of love
    That always had loved me,
So softly it rang out above —
    So wild and wanderingly.

O Voice, are you a golden dove,
    Or just a plain gray bird?
O Voice, you are my wandering love,
    Lost, yet forever heard!

Written in childhood.

CHRISTMAS EVE SONG

The earth was deeply laden,
  The moon shone very bright;
With Joseph was a maiden,
  Around her head a light.

That night to her was given
  The babe of Bethlehem,
And at the hour of seven
  He heard a little lamb.

What shall his name be, Mary?
  His name is Christ the Lord!
Then every dancing fairy
  And angel Him adored.

—

THE BROOK

O little rushing, roaring brook
  That runs through field and wood,
At all the little birds you look,
  At every child that's good.

There in the fields the sunbeams dance
  Upon your rippling sands,
And in the wood I see you glance
  Where the tall pine tree stands.

Written in childhood.

4

THE LINGERING DAY

The first bright star, the last slow bee,
The afterglow behind the tree,

The garden just about to fade,
The dog's last bark down through the glade,

The cricket's never-ending peep,
The little birds all fast asleep,

The little lambs' bleat and the old,
The cow's moo ringing soft yet bold,

All these I love and many more —
All lingering daylight and its lore.

—

THE WIND'S GOOD-NIGHT SONG

The stars are shining bright,
The birds in their nests tucked tight;

The little black cricket sings,
The far away church bell rings,

And we to sleep must go,
For the winds whisper low: —

"Go to sleep, go to sleep,
Till rosy dawn doth peep
Over the green hill tall:
            Good night,
            Sleep tight,
    Good night to all!"

Written in childhood.

O dream, what are you? —
　　A fairy or a sprite,
A goddess in the air,
　　Or just a flash of light?

A sudden flash of joy
　　That brightens up my mind,
Till wonders I see now
　　When first I was so blind.

—

Written in childhood.

NIGHT

Night, night, let down your hair
　　And shut away the stars.
Veil the moon in widowed grayness,
　　My soul is sad with care.

Night, night, be deep in silence,
　　Hush the breeze's song,
Hold me to your breast more closely —
　　My soul's too vast alone.

Written in adolescence.

The wind rummaged in the gutter
Like a hungry dog at night,
Sniffing, pawing, turning over things,
Then gulping noisily with gluttonous haste
Gorging on some scrap of mold.

A little girl was curled upon the curb,
Her bare feet in the rancid mud
That oozed about the cracks,
Clotted with waste paper and decay.

The wind sniffed at her tangled hair,
Eyed it, touched it, turned it with his paw,
Then whimpered on
Nosing down the street.

Her head was nestled on her rounded arm,
Flushed with soft pulsing sleep.
Her dark long lashes,
Sleek and smooth,
Lay like petals on a silent pool,
And with her breath the rhythm of sweet dreams
Played on the foul night air.

Hungrily the starved wind howled
And searched in the huddled shadows —
Bayed at the glaring street light
That mocked him with its crass, cold eye:

"Hark ye, people, I am mad — mad — mad.
Ye know not what I mean,
Ye know not the glory of my madness.
You say the world is round;
I say it is a bleeding child
Bound with gold chains."

Written in adolescence.

High on a peak of limitless ascent
My soul stood magnificent —
Endless the spaces that lay beyond,
Fathomless below,
And far above the yet starless realms
That no man knows.

Silent, serene, subdued with beauty,
Gazed I on eternity —
And through the inevitable ages stood,
And knew no end to time.

A burning soul in a formless sphere
That melted into night,
I stood alone and knew no fear,
For I had faith in life.

—

Written in adolescence.

THE QUEST OF YOUTH

THE WIND OF BEING

The wind of high mountains
And the tireless sea —
The wet wind of being
Is blowing in me.

As clear as the torrent
That leaps from the crag,
As strong as the tempest
When the heavens sag —

From the springs of the morning
That gush from the sky,
Like a freshet descending
It sweeps from on high.

Uncurbed is its pathway
And glad is its sting,
And I leap like a stag
On the hills of the spring.

Cold unto numbness
My limbs in its blast,
But the flame of young courage
Leaps naked and vast.

Each sinew is teeming
With its torrent of will —
But the cave of my heart
Is warm — and still.

THE WELLING WORD

O gleaming, wonder-weaving word,
Whose welling life is heard,

Limpid, lucent, clear,
By the quickened inward ear!

Where is the wellspring whence you flow,
Ripple forth and grow

To image and to form
That breathes and moves, is quick and warm,

Arrayed in melodies of hue —
Amethyst and blue,

Gold and green and rose —
A chiming wonder-woof, that glows

And glistens like a butterfly,
Floats from earth to sky,

From sky unto the earth,
From the meadows before birth —

The star-flowered meadowlands that lie
Before us when we die:

A butterfly of cosmic fields,
Who sips the nectar heaven yields,

Flits and floats from star to star —
An angel — with ambrosia.

RED, RED HEART

Red, red Heart —
I would I were a wild stag
Upon a lonely heath,
I would I were a silent crag
Where a wild sea-gull is crying.

Red, red Heart —
I would I were a piercing cry
Lost among the hills,
The wailing tide that's running high
Where a wild sea-gull is flying.

Red, red Heart —
The stag has a wounded side,
The crag is rent in twain.
The cry is drowned in the drenching tide
And the wild sea-gull is dying.

—

Empty is the night.
A chill moon lights the hill.
Empty, the night —
And every leaf is still.

As the hollow cave,
Cursed with stagnant air,
Extinguishes the candle
And blots its golden flare —

So the night, forsaken,
Merciless and dread,
Engulfs the burning soul
And lays her with the dead.

O grave, where is the answer
Within your emptiness;
Night, where is the flame
Can brave your wilderness?

'Tis death which they do find
Who seek for life — the still
And boundless void where beats
The fearful heart of Will.

"**N**ay —
Begone — I will not! —
All the fetters of the world I fling away.
I will be free, God!
I will be free, I say.

"From loneliness didst thou create me,
Lonely I will remain;
Thy heavens are a sea of darkness,
Thy earth a desert plain.

"A tempest of pent passions
And imprisoned powers are here
Battling within this bosom
Midst cries thou canst not hear:

"Fires of leaping lightning,
Ice with aching sting,
Slender yearning tendrils
Pregnant with the spring:

"Sublime, majestic mountains
Chiseled into space,
Wingéd angels stooping
With unwearying grace:

"These are the turbulent world
Illumined by my flame
Where I wander forever homeless,
A nomad without name.

"I am my own kingdom
And I my own king.
I am the fiery lightning,
I the icy sting.

"God — I renounce thee!
Empty is thy name,
For all to me is darkness
Save my lonely flame."

. . . .

Breathlessly I listened,
Listened with quivering tears —
A voice through the tingling silence
Fell softly through the spheres:

"Child — I am the flame.
Whom wouldst thou deny?
Thou art a word from off my lips —
And when thou speak'st — 'tis I."

—

TO COLOGNE CATHEDRAL

O sinewed shrine of man's desire
Of fire and ashes made,
Pealing organ of the mind —
Vibrant, stark, yet staid!

Creature of the pulsing ages
Vertebrate with pain,
How can I fathom through thy beauty
The groping soul who, slain,

Leapt into frail and perfect grandeur,
Yearning, cold as steel,
Trembling naked in God's tempest —
The form you now reveal!

O unity that breaks with union,
Strength that weeps in pain,
Mighty symphony of balance
Frail as frozen rain!

Crush not my being into cinders,
Nor too sharp my spirit rend —
Dumb, in stunned communion, kneeling,
I seek to comprehend. —

Man, thy spirit is too mighty,
Thy wisdom is too pure,
For thy dumb, crawling, blinded self
To face thee — and endure.

The Maid — the Maid — the Maid in the Moon
Sings songs to her silver lyre,
And lures me towards her phantom ship
Of shadow-grey and fire.

She leans from her port-hole window high
And combs her shining hair,
And sings me songs of sailing gladness. —
I wish I might be there!

—

HUMAN HEARTS

Roses in the snow,
Blood-red roses grow

In the crystal pain
Of the frozen rain.

Crimson blossoms bright
In a meadow white,

Burning hearts that bloom
In a crystal tomb,

Roses mid the thorns of birth
On the pallid brow of earth . . .

Bleeding feet have trod the snow
Where the human roses grow.

"I"

Within my heart
There is a sphere
Vast, illumined,
Clear.

Its might
Encompasses the stars.
It knows not space
Nor bars.

Within its depths
Of silent flame,
I found my secret
Name.

There at the core,
Like the first spark
That lit the face
Of dark,

With folded wings —
Unflinchingly,
"I" looked
At me.

POWERS OF DARKNESS

Dark winds sweep over the world;
The souls of men are torn, and hurled
Into the depths, where life is rent,
Blinded and burdened, bruised and bent
By the weight of the earth — the weight of death.

Dark mists sweep over the land;
The hearts of men grow faint to stand
Still and strong on the lonely peak
Where all is void, and the limbs are weak
With the pain of the boundless gulf beneath.

Death rules; but out of the deeps,
Out of the earthquake, fire leaps;
Out of the yawning gulf of woe,
Purging flames of vision glow,
And souls are forged by the Hand of Fate.

—

Oh stay —
Say not nay —
Silent stranger!
Tell me of that night
When a child of light,
Lying helpless in a manger,
Saved the dying earth
From fatal danger.

THE FLAME IN THE SOD

Long ago a child was born.
　　"Holy!" spake the sod.
His brow was bright as breaking morn,
Crownéd with a wreath of thorn.
　　"Bléssed be Thy name!"
　　Sang the flame.

Clothed in sorrow, clad in clay,
　　"Holy!" spake the sod.
The glowing eye of Cosmic Day
Lowly in a manger lay.
　　"Bléssed be Thy name!"
　　Sang the flame.

From the womb of winter earth,
　　"Holy!" spake the sod.
Out of darkling gloom and dearth,
Spring Eternal leapt to birth.
　　"Bléssed be Thy name!"
　　Sang the flame.

From the cradle-crypt of death,
　　"Holy!" spake the sod.
A voice of luminous silence saith —
"I am the immortal breath."
　　"Bléssed be Thy name!"
　　Singeth the flame.

THE BEAST

Where do you prowl
In the bottomless sea,
Beast of brute being,
O monster in me?

I will hunt you, will know you,
Discover your lair —
Stalk you through jungles
And wastes of despair.

You grin through the dark
Like a ghost from the tomb
And vanish again
In the fathomless gloom.

You cannot forever
Elude me and glide
Into the unknown abyss —
For there I will follow you
Into the pit
Where passion and woe
Are welded and knit,
Through gulf and through grave —
God grant me the will —
And the sword that I bear
Has the power to kill.

O beast of brute being,
Base monster in me,
Where do you prowl
In the bottomless sea?

Oh, I know the road to heaven
And it leads first down through hell,
Where the hound of hate lies crouching
And the tides of terror swell.

On the lonely road to heaven
The black mists loom and rise
In vast malignant masses
To a mountain waste of lies.

On the narrow road to heaven
There the serpent gleams and glides
And laughs within his belly
In the jungle where he hides.

Oh, I know the road to heaven
And the beasts that ravage there —
And the mighty Angel standing
Upon the lowest stair!

—

Cold, quiet dawn —
You cut the dark
With icy blade,
And kindle clear
The blue orb of heaven.
Day —
With dread clarity
Speaks through the world,
Waking the wilderness
With light —
Wherein no beast may hide.

A bitter fruit was on the tree
And an Angel gave it me.

I ate the rind, the core, the whole,
The seed I planted in my soul.

I planted it with toil and pain.
The Angel gave it sun and rain —

Until one day a shining blade
Pierced the sod where it was laid;

And lo, a sword of splendor grew
Up into the breadths of blue —

A plant of heaven, tall and bright,
It blossomed in a star of light.

—

Song of the growing grasses,
Cry of the bud in birth,
Eyes of opening flowers
Like stars from the dark of earth.

Dews of drenching sunlight,
Warmth of awakening spring —
Land that's young with laughter
And parts her lips to sing.

Gentle sun in heaven,
How beautiful to see
Are the growing grasses
Fed with milk from thee.

NEW MOON

Heavenly chalice held on high,
Slender moon in the summer sky!

Soft — the fading sunset gleams,
Hushed — the world in worship dreams.

Heavenly chalice, slim and pale,
Chalice of the Holy Grail,

Holding high the hidden light
Of the Sun's celestial might —

Dark, your bowl, but bright and fair
Heaven's treasure hidden there.

—

A seedling in the dark of earth
Cried aloud in pain of birth.

God looked down and gently said:
"By the earth is heaven fed." —

Later when the seedling grew,
Bloomed and faded, then it knew: —

By the suffering of the root
Angels reap the ripened fruit.

A FAIRY TALE

Fairy figures, glad and gay,
Glisten on the garden way —
Glisten, glimmer, gleam and play,
Blithely in the dawning day.

Fairy forms so frail and fleet,
Fairy folk with twinkling feet,
Gleefully they nod and greet
Gathering the dew to eat. —

Once there lived a mortal child.
The fairies fed her honey wild,
Fed her dew and myrtle mild,
Led her by the hand and smiled;

Led her to a forest glen,
A mossy bank beside the fen
Near the lurking lion's den,
Far from haunts of mortal men.

And there they showed her treasures bright,
Hidden in the gloom of night —
Treasures golden with a light
Never seen by mortal sight.

And there they sang to her a song,
An ancient legend, strange and long,
Of life and death, of truth and wrong,
About a hero, young and strong.

For seven days and seven nights
They sang of weird and wondrous sights —
Sang of depths and sang of heights,
Sang of heaven's starry lights;

And there they left her, lost and lone,
With her head upon a stone.
When she woke, with pain and moan,
Lo — she was a woman grown.

— — —

But still the fairies, glad and gay,
Glisten on the garden way —
Glisten, glimmer, gleam and play,
Blithely in the dawning day!

—

THE LUTE OF LIFE

Ash and flame, sand and dew,
Ever build the lute anew.

Star and sun and seraph wings
Play upon the tautened strings.

From the dark and hollow grave
Tidal music, wave on wave —

Sound and silence, shade and shine,
Body of a life divine;

Lute of earth with human strings —
Upon the cross the spirit sings.

Strong —

Let my heart be strong,
O hidden, flaming choir!
To bear your limpid fire.

Swift —

Let my limbs be swift,
To follow your fleet pace
Along the desert sands of space.

Bright —

Let my head be bright,
Awake with myriad eyes,
To probe your terrifying beauty
Behind the starlit skies.

—

THE SECRET IRON

OF THE HEART

Only the warmth we have given
Remains
When the heart is riven.

Only the joy that we share
Is balm
For despair.

Only the light that we spend
Can mend
What passions rend.

Bold mountains,
carve me with your rugged might,

give me the power to stand —
one with the wide, firm land;

will to fight
through weight of granite night —

breaking aloft,
to rise

with quiet, carven thought
into the crystal height
of starry skies.

Girdled with glacial flow,
mantled with silent snow,
grant me the power to grow

out of the bosom of the earth,
mounting with mighty birth,

a sun-lit pyre of sculptured form,
unshaken
in the wild clash of the storm, —

up to the high, clear blue,
O mountains,
patient — steadfast — like you.

THE ANGEL OF DESTINY

I wandered by the dark, interminable tide
And heard the hidden crooning of the deep;
Oh, fold me in your foam-bright arms,
Take me to your breast,
For I would sleep! —
But one,
Swooping low,
Cried
"No! —
Onward — where the storm bursts high,
And tumult wakes the turbid dark,
Onward — I bid you go!" —

I walked amid the hush of innumerable trees,
By the sweet, cool laughter of a stream;
Oh, let me rest in your green gladness
Amid your gracious leaves,
For I would dream! —
But one,
With startling blow,
Thundered
"No! —
Into the wilderness of stone
Where the dragon feeds on men,
Yonder — go!" —

I scaled the sunlit summit of a mighty mountain peak,
And my soul was eager as an eagle's wing;
Oh, let me live forever
Upon your windy height,
For I would sing! —
But one,
Like glacial snow,
Whispered
"No —
Down — into the dark abyss
Where truth is born of woe —
— Go!" —

Only the eye unwont to weep
May gaze beneath the sea of sleep,
Deep — Deep —
Within a deadly place,
Upon that awful, ancient face,
Terrible with mute disgrace —
Ashen as the lifeless coal —
Of sin within the soul.

Only the eye without a tear
May gaze upon the face of fear,
Clear — clear —
As carven stone,
Whereon is writ in shriveled bone —
"Man — thou must atone!
I am the sentry at the gate
Leading to the land of fate."

—

After the blast has cast its blight
And covered the grave with a garment white,
After the fire with scarlet thirst
Has seared the shroud of one accursed,
And truth has torn the veil of sleep
Until the awful, boundless deep
Has drunk up all the naked soul
And pain has purged the whole: —

When death has gathered up his own
And laid it underneath the stone,
When heaven's thief has siezed his prey
And borne the mortal self away —
Lo, from out the gulf of night,
The living, awakening Word of Light
Walks the earth with feet of flame,
Speaks into the void His heart and His name —
And the sound of His voice is eternal youth,
Is life and is love, the way and the truth.

Into the cold clutch of death,
the cruel hollow of the grave,
Your glowing glory poured
its living love, its leaping light —
and out of night,
the sun-bright infant
of my heart was born.

Your voice filled all the world,
and in Your heart
all life,
all sorrow, joy and hope
were held —
transmuted, cleansed
and through
Your vast compassion
born anew.

Your glory spoke,
Your living language shone;
I knew —
O Thou, Who only art
the all-outpouring heart
of the eternal tone —
Thine infinite bright Being
as mine own.

For without Thee
I were the child of death,
my being but a hollow shell,
my heart — a stone.
In Thee alone
is life —
the love that makes us whole,
the light that wakes the soul.

And from this hour
I learned to love the earth —
Thy body, grave and star;
to walk its ways
with wakening wonder
and resolve;
and first to grasp
with grateful hand and heart
my own humanity.

THE STRONG

What a fragile thing is strength!
How ephemeral its form!
For its gentle grace,
compassionate and warm,
is partner of its power.
And we may haste our pace,
or probe the hidden deep —
yet how few can reap
the bounty of an hour.

For strength eludes the bold,
defeats the quest of pride,
shatters the sharpest sword
and casts the bits aside.
And if we hold it bound,
it pales and slips away
without trace or sound.
'Tis fleeting as the dew —
mighty as the day —
and there are very few
who find its hiding place,
who meet it face to face.

The proud who boast its glory
perish at its hand.
But the weak who stand
alone, in mortal pain —
out of grief — attain
to vision of man's stain,
his guilt and bitter wrong,
delusion and delay,
to knowledge of decay — —
the mystery of death,
the secret of the breath.
And the weak are strong
when they live again
in the light of truth,
requickened by its ray.

Oh, strength is frail and tender —
elusive — and as slender
as a gossamer in spring.
Yet no hand can break it,
no tide nor tempest shake it,
and it conquers everything.

THE SECRET IRON

Let me not falter
in defeat,
nor alter
in the fevered heat
of circumstance,
but undismayed,
seizing the will to know,
with one, clean blow,
sever the rock of chance;
break the dark shroud apart
and free the metal at its heart —
moulding the living, molten ore
to a sharp, bright blade
of thought.

Quiet and unafraid,
as iron in the flame is wrought
to cool at length
with keener strength,
so mould me, mighty Master,
in the white heat of disaster.

In fires of undoing
and denial,
forge with living art
the secret iron
of my heart.
In burning trial,
temper the bright metal
of my will.
With faultless skill,
hammer the gleaming contours
of clear thought —
delicate, exact —
upon the anvil
of unalterable fact.

LEADERSHIP

As highest virtue in a leader
I value self-restraint —
the power to hold another's freedom
unimpaired;
to lay the words of wisdom at men's feet,
and yet have strength to meet
without complaint
the slings of ignorance and hate;
condemn untruth with righteous wrath,
yet hold the narrow path;
cherish each man as friend,
nor cease to spend —
and when the bread is shared,
command the courage
and the selfless skill
to view another's fate
and grievous folly,
yet, for freedom's sake,
use not a feather's weight
to influence his will.

For he alone is leader
who is a reader
of men's hearts,
and yet can hold,
holy and untold,
the secrets each imparts —
who harbors no will to rule,
but simply is a tool
and servant of the truth.

For there is no goal —
no power
planted in man's soul —
more precious in his sight
than freedom:
the tree of light
rooted in the starry height
above,
its flower —
love.

BENEATH
THE SCULPTOR'S HAND

As the wash of mighty waves,
pounding with hollow roar,
moulds the jagged outline
of the rocky shore —
so the long, dark waves of pain,
breaking with pent power
from out the boundless main
upon the promontories of your will,
have worn with enigmatic skill
the headlands of your eager soul;
moulded opposing masses
to one noble whole;
carved the conflicting contours
with consummate art;
mellowed the ardent power
of your impulsive heart.

For sorrow is a sculptor of the soul,
seizing mysterious tools
to serve his goal.
And the blow that wounds and brands
may be the chisel in his hands,
carving some imperfect part
of his immortal work of art.
So let no bitterness distort
or scar his mighty work;
let not impatience lurk
in hidden hollows of the heart.
But quietly beholding
the living forms unfolding
beneath the power of his hand,
awake at last to understand
the boundless glory of his goal,
as a free, creative soul.

For L.N.

OPEN SEA

I sail into an open sea,
into distant mystery;
yet the wind that sweeps along
laden with a virile song,
the wide uncharted waste,
the waves' unwearying haste,
the tide's deep melody,
are not strange to me.

For clad within the shroud
of tide and star and cloud,
Beings, powerful and wise
with clear, all-seeing eyes,
guide my tiny bark
through hazard, storm and dark. —

And though I sail alone
and hear the vast deep — moan;
yet their company is great,
those who guide my fate.
Their companionship is near;
their silent intimacy, dear.

And courage kindles in my heart.
I am content to sail apart,
borne within the boundless grace
of their passionless embrace.

—

FOR A NEW-BORN CHILD

The stone that slumbers in the earth,
The dreaming blossom on the bough,
The birds and rabbits in the wood,
The busy bee, the patient cow;
The lion, leaping fierce and bold,
The soaring eagle in the height,
The snow-white lambkin in the fold,
And all the great, wide, sun-lit world
Give you greeting, baby bright,
Wish you wisdom, power, joy,
    You tiny, infant boy!

The ways of this great earth
Are wise and beautiful —
Albeit rough and long.
The ways of man are mighty, gloriful —
Though heaped with wrong;
Wrought of woe and wonder,
Of suffering and song,
Ways of knowledge, love and hope,
Hammered in the heart's clear heat.
For long ago a star-bright baby
Trod the earth with tender feet,
Held within His heart the Sun —
The bright, all-gracious, mighty One —
Walked the ways of death and night
To wake the world with living Light.
And now the heavenly host on high,
And all things that live and die,
Praise His Name and mortal birth —
And He walks with every child
    Who comes upon the earth.

For B. v.Z.

—

This pain, that wakes my heart —
breaking in the silent dark
like a rising tide from out the wide
deep sea
of moving destiny,
is but a part
of that long birth
men call the life on earth.
For this strange thing
called suffering,
when planted in the human heart,
is but a seed,
laden with the need
of growth, that bursts apart
the narrow soul,
seeking the light and wonder of the whole;
striving with soft, bright leaves aloft,
to bloom as conscious deed
at last —
rooted in the fallen ashes
of the past.

Walking in a wood
at break of day,
I met an Angel
and asked my way.

He smiled, and pointed . . .
A slender ray
of sunlight fell
with magic spell,
and turned the cold,
indifferent clay
to living gold.

With childish grace
he raised his head,
and looking gravely
in my face
he said: —

"There is
but one road
to freedom —
be it trod
in age
or youth;
one winding path
to knowledge;
one door
to truth.

"And whosoever
takes this road
bears on his back
himself —
as load.

"Whatever mortal
seeks to tread
this winding path
must join the dead —
must journey through
a land of wrath,
mire and mud,
fire and flood,

and walk, at last,
through his own heart's
blood.

"And he who opens
that small door
shall gaze with awe
into his own heart's core;
and entering
that small,
bright place,
meet —
himself — there,
face to face."

And when I looked
once more,
the gold was gone —
the Angel, too.
But it was dawn!

—

The victory of one,
Beset with bitter pain —
Who loves the Sun,
And bears the ceaseless rain
Of suffering's sharp spears
With silent gallantry,
Unto the heart appears,
In moving majesty,
More beautiful, more bright,
Than aught the eye can see —
Flooding earth and height
With healing melody.

Oh, how deeply blest are we
Who are privileged to see
Such human victory!

For L.H.

SONG

My heart is like a wild bee
    Buzzing in the briar;
My heart is like the high, bright heaven,
    Full of quiet fire.

The lilacs and the lilies
    Are a glory to behold,
For the morning dew has dressed them
    In a garment all of gold.

The stream beyond the garden
    Is gurgling with glee,
Telling tales of wonder
    To the trailing willow tree.

The merry little minnows
    Dance nimbly in and out,
And up the sparkling waterfall
    Leaps a speckled trout.

Beyond the far, blue mountains
    Fleece-white cloudlets lie,
Like sleeping, new-born children
    In the summer sky.

Oh, my heart is like a wild bee
    Buzzing in the briar;
My heart is like the high, bright heaven,
    Full of quiet fire.

Bright Angel, who bends ever watchful above me,
Husht in your starlight I harken and start
With wakening awareness to sense how you love me,
Gazing so silently into my heart —

How patiently, surely, you secretly guide me,
Admonish and mother my stumbling ways.
When I thought in my erring and anguish to hide me,
I slept in the glow of your sheltering gaze.

O bright one above me, though earth-dark may blind me,
I sense in my heart the sight of your eyes
And know in their answering gaze I shall find me,
Shall wake in their full glance one day — and arise!

—

What shall I do,
Who wander here alone?
Tread tenderly the sod
And love the humble stone.

What shall I live for,
Although none may care?
To make a human offering
Of every breath of air.

What shall I be then,
Who myself am naught?
A clear, awakened organ
For the light of thought.

ONLY

Only
the lonely
are led
to the threshold
of sight.

Only
the dead
can tread
the ocean
of light.

Only
the living
are fed
the bread
of the night.

Only
the fallen
can lift
their head
and heart
to the height.

—

THE HAND
OF THE WORKMAN

The myriad, wise, all-seeing stars
That lie beneath us and above
Hold us in their vast embrace
Of selfless love.

Though darkness threaten us with fear
And bitter be the night —
In the cosmic heavens the sun
Sheds unceasing light.

The workman's hand is firm of grip and good to feel,
An instrument of mind and heart and will.
The deeds of ages flow from every finger tip
With expeditious ease as human skill.

It is a selfless thing of humble strength and habit,
It's very being but to serve and do.
And yet its cunning conjures spirit into form;
Its ministrations mould the earth anew.

Though it has might to move and shape the weight of mountains,
'Tis from a tender tool such magic flows.
In delicacy, form and hue its facile fingers
Are as fragile as a wild five-petaled rose!

—

When pain of error leaves its open wound,
There thought can enter in, to touch the heart
With golden fingered light, ere it has swooned
To see its own blood flow — and with such art,
As only star-born beings can achieve,
Can cause that sleeping crimson stream of life
To glow most wondrous clear, and to conceive
Within its depths, where turmoil, woe and strife
Are found, the young bright power of will that grows
With tranquil inner strength beneath its light
To put forth radiant petals as a rose —
A blood-red blossom born out of the night.
        When every wound becomes a scarlet flower,
        The heart is sheltered in a starry bower.

SKY-COOL WATER!

Bursting tides of cosmic anger
Swallow mountain, lake and hill;
Lightning strikes into the valley,
Wind and torrent have their will.

With majestic, primal grandeur
Heaven shakes the listless earth,
Pours forth with divine impatience
Foaming freshets of rebirth.

"Come, ah come," the streams are calling
As they hasten toward the sea.
"Breathe, ah breathe, with me more deeply,"
Sighs the great, green maple tree.

Ah, what strong, what rich aroma
Rises from the furrowed land.
"Drink, oh drink, the sky-cool water —
Drink — and understand."

Oh, to drink life's healing nectar
From the bursting storms of fate,
Drink like you its fresh, cool wonder . . .
Beauty — in its primal state!

'MID BUTTERCUPS

Amid a thousand cups of gold
All lifted high
To catch the laughing light
Of heaven's eye,
Yet never full, the more they hold,

A silent, snow-white butterfly —
An elfin queen,
Who dances on the breeze
Through gold and green —
Comes gliding tremulously by.

Absorbed, from one to one she floats
And pauses long
To sip their honeyed light,
While limpid song
Comes rippling forth from wingéd throats.

A fresh wind stirs the trees,
The forest sighs . . .
In peaceful ecstasy
The meadow lies
Amid the blissful hum of bees,

Where chaste and white, the butterfly
Sips the light
And flutters on her way . . .
A gracious sight
To see such wonder wander by —

Amid a thousand cups of gold
All lifted high
To catch the laughing light
Of heaven's eye —
A thousand brimming buttercups of gold!

FOR FELICITAS

I brought a blossom to her side
Where she lay in hush of death —
When lo, she woke, and starry-eyed
Gazed about with bated breath.

Her fragile body, foot and limb
Were arch and pillar to her glance,
A temple of the Cherubim —
And she was free to run and dance.

Her tip-toes hardly touched the ground
So light and free she sped along
Into the garden where she found
Her mother, mid the amsel's song.

Two evil ones waylaid her path.
But swift, her guardian at her side
Cast them down with golden wrath
And trod them low beneath his stride.

So all untouched she takes her way
With moon-bright gown and flowing hair.
The wingéd beasts in bright array
Have taken her into their care.

—

A hush of wonder
wakes the weary, waiting world.
The stars draw near,
like innumerable eyes of children,
inviolate and clear.

O heavenly children of the height,
light
with the bright
wisdom of your gaze
the stiff, cold corpse of thought;
awaken,
with your gleaming rays,
the living World-Thought-Beings
from their chill, dark grave!

FOR MARION MORSE MACKAYE

Commanding was the courage of her face,
scupltured by the frozen tides of death,
image of inexorable truth —
immensely strong and resolutely brave . . . .

See — in the sheltering candle-shine — she smiles!
Gracious peace has stolen o'er her features,
growing ever deeper, gentler, brighter
as the hours take their silent pace . . . .

Like a Grecian hero, as of old —
her wondrous hair, like clouds of mystery
and glory, sweeping upward from her brow —
it seemed she strode with eager virgin vigor
over mountain-tops at break of day . . .

a glad young goddess, gracious and serene,
the cross that leads to life upon her breast —
about to start upon her starward way,
to wander forth into the fields of love — —
out into the pastures of the Day . . . .

—

Silent, silent as the grave
Let me learn to be —
Silent as the homeless wave
That sinks into the sea.

For the surface cannot say
The sorrow of the deep.
Darkness cannot tell the day
Of the gulf of sleep.

Neither can these lips of earth
Clothe the heart with speech,
Capture in the robes of birth
The deeds which death can teach.

Yet if mute the Word be born
From the breaking heart,
As the young shoot bursts the corn
— Silence blooms in Art.

SO MUCH

There is so much that I would do,
So much I long to give to you,

I think I could not bear the weight,
The sorrow of this unsolved fate

That took you from your house of clay
While we had still so much to say,

Did I not know that we shall meet,
That once again our eyes shall greet

And kindle with an answering light;
That like the swift unerring flight

Of homing pigeons loosed on high
By angels' hands from out the sky —

Guided by the stars of birth,
In another life on earth,

We who once were child and mother
Shall meet again and know each other,

And I shall have the chance to do
All that I would do for you.

For M.M.M.

—

We only learn the suffering of death
Who live — crumbling into dust as one who dies;
For all that's small in us must suffer death
In order that the great in us may rise.

We only learn the majesty of death
Who, crumbling — are caressed by Spirit might
That rises up on wings of cosmic breath
Above the hollow anguish of our night.

WORLD WAR

Let us take each other's hands
At this midnight hour of strife —
Turn our faces toward the lands
Where the dead arise to life.

Round the world dense clouds of death
Shroud the earth in crimson snow,
Loose their storms of stinging breath,
Wrap their winding sheet of woe.

At each step a chasm gapes —
Boundless crater of distress.
Though we see not — none escapes
The anguish of its emptiness.

Like vile vapours from foul graves,
Vast demonic hordes conspire —
Marshal men to be their slaves —
Make the earth their dread empire.

Yet above the fields of blood,
There, the dead look down — and say:
"Christ is risen from the flood —
Walks the tides of cosmic day.

"His still voice alone can waken
Human hearts from sleep of sense.
When the roof-beams of the world are shaken,
He alone is your defense.

"In the meekness of His power
All the demons must despair —
Like a humble hedge-rose flower
Amid briars — love is fair.

"With the free gaze of your heart
Look the demons in the eye.
They will cower and depart
And the angels fill the sky.

"For the humble will find gladness,
The fearless will find light.
Out of all the seas of sadness,
The spirit will take flight.

"Everything on earth must alter —
Pain and death redeem the past.
Oh, take heart and do not falter —
He is with you to the last."

So amid the woe of war,
Like the silent fall of dew,
Those upon the starward shore
Ever speak to us anew.

Day and night the dead are near,
They who reap the fruit of pain.
Let us heed them, let us hear —
That their death be not in vain.

—

BLUE FLOWER

Blue flower, blue flower,
Deep-eyed dew-flower,
Here in your earth bower,
Where is your home?

Out of what ocean
Ever in motion,
Sea of devotion,
Did you just come —

Gazing so far-eyed,
Watching so star-eyed
Fairy forms, far and wide,
Fleeter than foam?

Is it the sea of light,
Kindling our spirit-sight,
Flooding our form with might
Where e'er we roam?

Is it the same deep
Whither we go in sleep,
Well, whence our hearts weep,
Heaven's blue dome?

Blue flower, true flower,
Clear-eyed dew-flower,
Deep in my heart's bower,
Here is your home!

FOR THE DEAD

You sail upon the sea of years,
Homeward, toward the shores of birth,
Upon the deep blue waves of tears,
Amid the misting spray of mirth.

You sail upon the sounding deep
Through all the wonder you have won,
Retraversing the tides of sleep,
Guided by the dawning sun.

In a moon-bright barque you sail,
The hollow of an angel's wing,
Blown backward by a cosmic gale,
The winds of fate that sigh and sing

And bear you with their mighty speech,
The moving rhythm of their song,
The awful mysteries they teach,
Onward — on, across the long

Wide reaches of the astral sea
Where lurk the monsters of the past
Still unredeemed, while silently
Your Angel watches by the mast. —

But in his heart you weave your wish
And cast the net into the waves
And gather in the starry fish
That wake all sailors from their graves.

For since the great Gold Fish of Heaven
Sank into the depths below
And gave Himself as living leaven,
The fish of life begin to glow

And glimmer in the tide, where all
Who sail the ocean of the dead
May gather-in the wondrous haul
Of starry fishes, and be fed.

O MY ANGEL

O my Angel, spread your wings
And bear me to the source of things —

Far into the world of light
Hidden in the heart of night.

O my Angel, let me sleep —
Bathe me in the star-bright deep.

Bathe my being bright and clean —
Heal me in the vast unseen.

—

Are you the dead?
Who hover like soft sunlight
Round my bed,

Who warm the gloom
And flood with tender quietude
This chill, dark room,

And did you start
This silent flow of peace
Within my heart?

Oh, is it you:
Whom I so dearly love
And dearly knew.

Are you the dead?
"Oh no — love does not die,
We live!" they said.

As the single drop of water
Recreates the starry whole,
So the angels see their faces
In the mirror of the soul.

As the dew of morning sparkles
In the lily for a span,
So the deeds of angels glisten
In the mortal cup of man.

And as lightly as the lily
Is uplifted by the sun —
The human form arises
With the Resurrected One.

For the house which we inhabit
Has been built by master hands.
In and out its carven portals
Seraphs pass in starry bands.

In its dimly-lighted chambers
We may strive and brood alone,
Blind to beauty that surrounds us,
To the lords who laid the stone,

Blind to those who guard and tend us,
Bring us heaven's bread to eat,
Spread their rainbow-wings beneath us
To support our careless feet —

Blind to Him Who gives them being
Through His spirit's inmost breath —
Came Himself to purge the mansion
Of the pestilence of death.

Yet without His Hosts we humans
Would be void — a thing of naught.
In the hearts of sky-bright beings
We are born of cosmic thought.

As the single drop of ocean
Is at one with all its tides,
Deep within the breathing bosom
Of the gods the soul resides.

And the chalice of the body,
Like the lily in the sun,
Is uplifted by the glory
Of the Everlasting One.

—

In the still hush of the heart,
In a quiet all apart

From the hum and whirr of wheels,
From the marching tramp of heels

On the pavement by the door
Where the metal monsters roar;

Just the other side of here,
There's a place all bright and clear

Where a deep-blue flower is blowing
And a stream of peace is flowing

With cool rushes by the brink,
Where the sheep come down to drink;

Where the air is like a friend,
And the heavens seem to bend

With a look of virgin love
Ever watchfully above;

Where I too may come and drink,
Come and wander, come and think,

Come and find the deep-blue flower,
Breathe its all restoring power,

In the still hush of the heart,
In a quiet all apart.

The way — that led through parching frost,
Through lonely caverns of the lost,
Down through the valley of the damned —
That cruel, stifling canyon crammed
With wizzened, loveless hosts of doom
Who ravage in vain the empty tomb —
Has led at last to sweeter air,
To greening slopes and orchards, where
The hosts of heaven tend the land
And gently take me by the hand.

"See," they say — their child-like faces
Smiling with the sparkling traces
Of the starry paths they wander —
"In the darkling valley yonder
How the frosty creatures cower,
For your sight has quelled their power,
And the anguish of your heart
Has assuaged their rage — is part
Of a healing balsam, easing
Those they strangle with their freezing
Grim, inexorable clasp —
Who still slumber in their grasp.
See, their claws can rob you only
Of the cloak that makes you lonely,
Of the self that, craving wonders,
Only craves itself, till thunders
From the living deep have shaken
The dreaming star-child till it waken —
Wake and wander at our side,
Wander freely far and wide.

"Oh, come with us and do not fear,
The stars have need of comrades here,
Of wakeful toilers here below
To help the heavenly grain to grow —
Who till earth's dark, love-torn, alone,
And heal her anguish through their own.
Both hell and heaven need your seeing.
Oh, be for us a human being!
Take us all into your heart,
That so we may become a part
Of that new transfigured earth
Which quickens now for glad rebirth."

FOR MATHILDE SCHOLL

Oh, silence speaks a language
    More swift and true
Than mortal lips can utter,
    More perfect
    Than the dew.

Like a crystal stream
    In deep repose,
With clear untroubled current
    It sparkles
    As it flows.

Down deep glades of sorrow
    It oft must pass,
Through icy gulf and tempest,
    Or lonely,
    Deep morass.

Yet through cave, or starlight —
    How secretly
It stirs the soul and wakes it
    With hidden
    Melody.

A fount of flowing wonder
    From near and far,
It streams from stone and flower,
    From creature,
    Cloud and star.

From heart to heart it flashes
    Like breaking day,
A bond of understanding
    No tide
    Can sweep away.

O silent golden language,
    So swift and bright —
How closely you enfold us
    In your weaving
    Sea of Light!

Growing grasses, sinking sun —
So the summer day is done.

Gentle glory robes the sky,
Homing geese go winging by.

Evening wraps the meadow round
With the insects' choral sound.

From the marshes by the stream
Silver mists begin to gleam,

Like a freshening veil to grace
The fair young water's virgin face.

And from the trees just out of sight
Through the soft, oncoming night —

Hark! — the thrush's liquid note
Like wild honey from his throat:

Seek not ever more to do.
Be the voice that springs in you.

—

Lofty, all-loving One!
How lowly and small
Is the door to Your kingdom!
How oft we may fall
On the perilous pathway
Into the All.

For no humbler footpath
Is found on the earth,
Though it lead us through all
Of heaven's girth —
No entrance more meager
Than the flood-gates of birth.

Deep, deep within,
Dwells a silent one
With eyes that never close
And forehead like the sun.

O you, whose clear eyes gaze
Upon all I do,
Upon all I am,
Who, mute one, are you?

Then with strong, sweet voice
The sun-browed being spoke —
And at his gentle word
I trembled . . . . and awoke!

—

When the storming war-hordes threaten
To tear mankind apart,
Can you be quite still within you,
Whole within your heart?

When men build to save their brothers
Shelters bored in stone,
Can you find your brother's star
Shining all alone?

When the learnèd teach each other
To shape the human race,
Can you find man in God's image —
Look upon his face?

When the righteous ravage truth
Till no sod be found,
Can you tread where nothing is —
Freedom's fertile ground!

Oh, never more
let me believe, as oft before,
that I — who live and die,
whose heart beats high,
yet breaks and bleeds —
could merit virtue for my deeds.

For goodness dwells
alone in truth —
and softly wells
from out that secret, silent source
from which the Spirit takes its course —
flowing with the mighty,
all-refreshing force
and mystery of youth
into every being,
every form and grain,
every drop of rain,
given shape and birth
upon this ancient earth.

And we who covet virtue,
and claim its golden hue,
are like the drop of dew
that sparkles in the sun
and thinks itself the one
that shines and glows —
forgetting that its bright
unbidden beauty flows
with silent, selfless might
out of the distant height.

Yet man, with conscious sight,
perceiving his own light,
is gifted with the grace
and inward strength to trace
its source and origin —
and finally to win
- when fate has struck the hour -
the free, awakened power
to gaze at last upon the One
Who lights the world — the Risen Son —
and know himself a part
of His great, glowing heart.

Come! — Have we not enough of all this evil!
Do we not lie sleeping in rank mire!
And is it not mankind itself that is at stake?

Then let us in sheer wrath rise up within ourselves,
Sieze this torpor with both hands
And shake our swooning spirits mightily awake.

The beast whose dire destruction ravages the earth
Has dug his lair within our flesh
And tears his prey within the temple of the God.

Up then! — Draw the shining blade of consciousness.
Strike the monster to the heart,
And purge the edifice of man where Christ once trod.

—

Caught in the cross-tides of conflict,
          Calm
     Is the cradle of might.

Trapped in the dark of delusion,
          Wonder
          Gives light.

Blinded by the shell-fire of passion,
          Love —
     Awakens our sight.

To conquer the hordes of evil,
          Hearts
          Must bleed.

In the ravaged soil of destruction
          Sow
          The seed
     Of the free deed.

Oh let us learn to be
  Ever bigger than we are,
To hold the silent bounty
  Pouring from afar —
The glory round about us,
  Smiling star, on star, on star . . . . .

Oh let us learn to be
  Ever less than we have been,
Until at length from nothing
  Slowly we begin
To hear the loving language
  Uttered only from within.

Oh let us learn to give
  All that we at length would be,
That so the stars within us
  Become eyes to see —
And that loving language
  Set all beings free.

—

Daily, daily we must die —
Feel the pangs of parting from the earth,
Find the Spirit's secret bourne of birth
And waken — from on high!

—

FORGED IN SUN

Is not the meaning of mankind
Writ on the walls of the heart,
Writ there in luminous writing,
Causing the spirit to start?

For the walls of the heart are as wide
As the spirit can wander afar,
And the writing is written as clear
As the steadfast eye of a star;

And one who can enter that chamber,
As wide as the spirit can wing,
May read there the meaning of mankind,
Which causes all heaven to sing!

Are we not all woven like bright blossoms
With strands of light into one flowering wreath —
Those of us who breathe the breath of heaven
And those who breathe the naked air beneath.

So like one unfading cosmic garland,
So firmly, ever newly intertwined,
We weave the life-web of the seamless garment
Of the spirit being of mankind.

—

We met upon an inward path
At the full of day,
Met upon a clear, small path
Pursuing the same way,
Met upon a pathway flooded
By an inner sun,
Bound upon a spirit quest
Long ago begun . . .
A pathway woven of awareness,
Woven firm and bright,
With soil of understanding wrought
Out of the heart's own sight.

It beckons gladly on afar
And glimmers from the past,
Where it has wound through other lives
To lead us here at last,
In quest of that true trust and freedom —
The core of human kind —
That inmost, sacred spirit kernel
It is man's goal to find.
The living-dead who walk with us,
They smile and lead the way —
The spirit-sun enfolds us all
In its gentle day.

For K.E.

When on his spirit-journey man himself meets man . . .
Then through the temple of the human being sounds
A cry, a call — like a clear burst of organ tone —
       Awake!   —   Awaken!
Until the whole great citadel is shaken,
Is stirred and startled to its smallest living stone,
And from its groundwork to its vaulted dome resounds: —
O man, within your temple, waken unto man!

—

The times are full of tears.
The days are dark
With pent impending storm. —
It thunders!   —   Hark! —

What heart-torn voice entreats
Beneath its roar?
What bleeding rose-red speech
From spirit core

Blooms on ebon boughs
To spend unbidden
Its fragrance on the bitter air
And — as from hidden

Thorny dark, bright blossoms
Are unfurled —
Utters love and healing
To the world!

There is a land of inner sun,
A virgin land of inmost day,
Where men may meet and make their way
Upon a journey long begun.

A fragile, firm unfettered place —
So near, yet ever just apart —
Where men may greet with waking heart
The one who bears their brother's face.

Where each may find what is his own,
Where one can tread on truth alone,
And freedom is the only air
For men to breathe who journey there.

—

Hear the trickling of the water!
The soft laughing of the brook!
There's a golden flower glinting
In the green ferns yonder, look!

A golden flower blooming
In the weaving light and shade
That builds a lofty temple
Of this green untroubled glade.

A golden blossom gleaming
In the sun-lit glade of man
By the stream of quiet, flowing
From the spring where life began.

A golden blossom smiling
In the meeting of our eyes,
In a temple that is vaster
Than the whole, wide, starry skies.

Did you not know that all that is human is holy,
That the living matrix of man
Is wrought of the substance of heaven?
In him is the starry plan,
And he alone is the leaven
Transmuting to beauty and goodness all that is lowly.

For he is the house of Him who is most high,
The secret chamber where
The gods ply alchemy;
In him the golden stair
They tread unceasingly
That heaven may know itself as you and I.

—

Yes, I hear,
Deep and clear,
Hear your being
Speaking, dear!

Oh, I feel,
Sharp as steel,
Feel the hazard
At your heel!

But I see,
Quietly,
How your Angel
Looks at me.

And I know
It is so —
Christ is with us
Where we go.

What great hand has fed us?
What tender hand led us
To meet this fleet hour,
To find this frail flower
Of bright petaled power
That blooms like a shower
Of joy on our way,
This sun-dappled day? —

While warm breezes play
In the leaf-spangled spray
Of the heavenly seas
That swirl through the trees —
And the glad honey bees
Are burrowing their knees
In bright pollen gold,
Taking all they can hold.

The seeds that were sown
Have sprouted and grown.
The young birds have flown.
The meadows are mown.
And each golden blade
Of hay has been made.
While there through this glade,
Half nestled in shade,

The long light is streaming,
The birches are gleaming,
Deep grasses are greening,
Soft elm branches leaning
Over the pool —
Quiet and cool
As the bourne of our soul,
Reflecting the whole.

What great hand has fed us?
What tender hand led us
To meet this fleet hour,
To find this frail flower
Of bright petaled power
That blooms like a shower
Of joy on our way,
This sun-dappled day!

—

We came in search of what is whole — the wholly human,
    In search of man in all his grief and grace,
Came here to find his archetypal form and beauty,
    To meet him and to greet him, face to face.

We came in earnest quest of him, in want — and sought
    In every mortal for some hidden trace,
Some clear, unclouded proof of him — a sign, a glint
    Of his glad smile, a hint of his free pace.

How often have we searched for him in breathless sorrow;
    How oft encountered merely men, or masks,
Or suddenly confronted strange, misshapen creatures.
    "Oh, where is he?" a voice forever asks.

But when from out another's soul his image looms —
    When, through the open doorway of the heart,
We glimpse his star-hewn stature in the sun-drenched air
    And meet his unveiled gaze, its welcome dart —

Ah — who then is more dear, more blessèd, or more fair!

We hold within our close clasped hands
A treasure which is God's and man's,

Enfold within our woven hearts
The source from which all Being starts.

And in the meeting of our eyes
The light of all creation lies.

—

So sure it is — O dearest one —
Though darkling storms may gather round
And still as wanderers we must roam,
In the land of inner sun
On love's imperishable ground,
Where truth is light, we have our home.

A home so still and warm and bright,
Built on a soil so firm, so fair,
So wide — all heaven is harbored there;
And yet right here on earth its light
Sheds its peace with sheltering care,
And healing blossoms everywhere.

For there a silent heavenly guest
Sups with all who share the bread
Of destiny and taste its wine;
Gives them nourishment and rest,
And with the wounds, where He has bled,
Wakes their eyes for the divine.

Oh, could I tell you, dear, the wonder,
The wonder of the dew,
The dew-drop on the thorn,
T'would spread before our glistening eyes
Our garden in the starry skies
Before we both were born.

Oh, could I bear for you the anguish,
The anguish of the thorn
That would become a rose,
T'would pierce our beings to the quick
And heal us by its barbéd prick
With the love that flows.

Oh, could I paint for you the beauty,
The beauty of the rose
That opens to the sun,
T'would fill us with such power of birth
To do the deeds of heaven on earth
That our feet would run.

Oh, could I sing for you the glory,
The glory of the sun
That glows within the heart,
T'would melt the clouds of death away
With all the grandeur of its day
And burst the tomb apart.

And could we open for each other
The secret of the heart,
The heart that bleeds upon the cross —
T'would turn the tomb into a bower,
The blood-drops would as roses flower —
Our starry garden sprung anew from loss.

As new
As the dew
Each dawn on the grass,
Is the will
That can do
Each deed as we pass.

As clear
As the tear
On the cheek of a child,
Is the heart
In which fear
Has melted and smiled.

As calm
As the palm
Of the hand of a god,
Is the healing
Of harm,
The redemption of sod.

As tender,
As slender,
As the sprout in the seed,
Is the hidden
Splendor
Of love's free deed.

—

A blessing haunts the wind,
Whispered in some far land,
In reverence of a faithful heart,
And some gentle hand.
It brushes softly past me
As it travels on its way,
And leaves behind a fragrance
Whose freshness seems to say: —
"Blessedness is beauty,
And a blessing is a truth
As steadfast as the morning star,
Ever radiant with youth."

Through the breathless, restless dark of outer downfall,
Like deep chiming,
Dear,
I hear you —

On the icy windswept cliffs of inner conquest
Where we're climbing,
Here,
I'm near you —

In the lonely, lifeless void, through anguished wastes,
What voice is rhyming
Clear: —
"Don't fear you!" —

From the deathless dark
A star
Is singing —
On the frozen cliffs
A rose
Is springing —
Through the pathless void
A child
Is bringing —

A ripened fruit,
A golden flute,
An oaken spade,
Which Christ has made.

The pasture grasses bend beneath the breeze
Who walks with velvet slippers o'er the land.
A salt sea-song she whispers to the trees
And leads the fair-haired sunlight by the hand.

They walk with such a free and gracious stride
Across the glistening billows of the grass
That move with them in one on-sweeping tide,
As each blade bows its head to see them pass.

So fair, they walk, so fervently and free,
That wheresoe'er they wend their eager way,
All bow in homage — grass and shrub and tree.
Can we as mortals then do less than they?

—

Let your hand not hurt
The flower it would give.
Let your tongue not mar
The words of love that live

As angels in your heart. —
For the rose is crushed
By too firm a grasp,
The angel's voice is hushed

By too blunt a tongue,
By too sharp a breath. —
Let the Word itself
Arise in you from death.

The dew is twinkling in the grass.
The bluettes eyes are bright.
The daisies look into the sun
And laugh for sheer delight!

The black-eyed-susans by the lawn
Are just a mass of gold;
And in the orchard cherries hang
Like jewels to behold.

The wind is singing in the trees
A gentle, happy song
And lays its head to rest awhile
Where the grass is long.

See there! Upon the old stone wall,
A chipmunk looks at me
With golden eye, as if absorbed
In some great mystery.

And through the air a butterfly,
With quiet outspread wings,
Comes floating by — so close! Is it
A message that she brings?

The sky is spotless overhead.
The kind, warm sun looks down
And takes the world into his arms,
And wraps it in a gown

All woven out of soft, warm strands
Of fleecy, sparkling light —
A gown all woven out of love
And heavenly delight.

And every creature, bird and beast,
Each flower, grass and tree,
Wrapt close within its warm bright folds
Whispers joyously —

"Oh we are clad in golden raiment,
The raiment of the sun!
In the spotless, seamless garment
Of the Risen One." —

Oh, I would lay my hand upon the heart
Of every man who grieves
And bid him hark! —
Hold his inmost breath
And wink his clouded eyes awake
Until he start
And tremble with quick joy . . .
Bid him be comforted! —

For see! All earth and air are flooded
As with a tender Easter dawn.
A sea of boundless love surrounds
And fills each being who is born —
Pours with gentle inward ardor,
Even as the springtide sun,
Enveloping each plant and creature,
Each lofty and each lowly one —

From the depths of man's own being
Flashes with unfathomed wonder,
Speaks to him like mountain water,
Or with the majesty of thunder
Flows like streams of star-plucked music,
Welling, sounding through his breast,
And at the bottom of all selfhood
Lies inexpressibly at rest. —

'Tis but the cramping, icy cloak
Of intellect, the winding sheet
Of our self-seeking, which enshrouds
The glory which we long to greet,
Proclaiming: — The earth is wholly altered!
- A star where life is won through loss -
It is the flesh and breathing being
Of Him Who hung upon the cross.

And we are wrapt and woven round
By His unbounded love which flowed
With His heart's blood on Golgotha
And dyed the earth until it glowed,
Began to gleam, to shed a glory,
Became the seedling of a sun,
Of a young light-woven earth,
The garment of the Risen One,

Who walked the earth — and died to be
The bounty of us all. — Oh, wake!
And start with awe — each human heart —
Fling wide your fettered door and take
The freshets of His breathing life
Deep, deep into your core,
Till there be none who does not know
Its healing — none who ever more

Can rest, till he find power to pour
The living waters forth again
From heart to human heart — until
They wash away each earthly stain,
Cleanse each wound and soothe each pain,
Transform the desert of man's brain
To fields of fresh eternal grain.

—

There's peace within the ripening grain,
Comfort in a drop of rain.

The one is food, the other drink —
The verities we breathe and think.

So frail the fruits of life appear,
No bigger than a falling tear;

The self, so small, it melts away
In the immensity of day.

And yet, like glistening dawn-fresh dew,
How unimaginably new

The will that bourgeons in each deed!
How immeasurable each seed

Of thought that springs to light,
Quickening the soul with sight.

The self is like a grain of heaven
Great with everlasting leaven.

Yet love is even vaster far
Than any of these others are.

How can I serve You, gentle Saviour,
Source and ocean of my being,
Eye and light of all my seeing,
Sun that quickens me from in me,
Breaks my wintry shell apart,
While 't is only You within me —
Goal and Guardian from the start.
How, oh how! fair Sun and Saviour
Can I speak from out my heart
The bounty You bestow upon me,
Can I serve You with that art
Which gives to love the love you give me —
Lives to love the life you live me!

—

TEMPERED IN TRUTH

How tender we must be
To see,
How unequivocally clear
To hear.

How silent we must grow
To know,
How meekly live
To give.

How true —
Inimitably new
Must be
Our love of Thee
To do.

How deep
Is the sleep
Of the gray world
Of our modern day-world,
The whirling pace
Of this mad race
Of our
Self-blinding greed for power.

How bright
Is the light
Of the far world
Of the infinite star-world,
The divine seeing
Of the hosts of heavenly being,
Whose might
Is the sheer light
Of their all-pervading sight.

—

Beneath the fevered rush
Of all this seething greed and grieving —
Within the brimming hush
And rhythmic weaving of heaven's breathing —
Touched by the virgin blush
Of silence, wreathing the face of Truth,
With that star-startling smile
And winning grace of youth —
Yet ever leaving, oh, so tenderly,
The child of man and atom
Free —

There with thee —
Borne on thy weightless ways,
Bathed in thy spaceless gaze
In sun-lit mystery —
Oh, vast Virgin Verity,
Let my heart be
Eternally.

WHO WILL SPEAK

In this atomic tyranny
Of blood and brains, who frames his speech
To leave both friend and foe so free
That manhold is evoked in each?

Who, in this bewildered hour
Of barbéd intellect and strife,
Can act out of the heart's full power,
Can forge and wield the fine-edged knife

Of steeled and tempered consciousness,
To utter words so true and sharp
That they can cut the emptiness, —
Can pierce, like tones plucked from a harp,

This stagnant moil of reeking air,
This farce of unreality,
That dupes the peoples to despair
And soddens their humanity?

Who can aim the heart's blade true
And cleave the taudry veil asunder;
With all his human stature, who
Can speak with lightning and with thunder —

Can walk erect, wide-eyed with death,
And waking, foil the wraiths of terror,
Can summon thoughts with living breath
To grapple with the hordes of error?

And when the faithful are accused,
The wise deserted and denied,
When the humble are abused,
The free beset from every side,

Who will speak in such an hour,
Who, in face of shame and death,
Will act out of the heart's full power,
Speak the truth with living breath?

How often we bemoan our fate
And claim that it is now too late,
We lack the talents, power, time
To write a forthright, moving rhyme.
We feel we are not granted force
To steer a sure uncharted course,
To knit our thoughts in free designs
And mould our lives on mighty lines.

But have we probed this plaintive stand,
Summoned sufficient clear command
To trace the lack through all disguise
And spot it where it really lies?
Perhaps it wears a plainer face,
Is reared in quite a different place
Far closer than we dare to think.

Can it be here upon the brink
Between delusion and deceit,
This thing that quails before our eyes —
This vain unwillingness to meet
Ourselves, and learn our ailment lies
Not in such ills of our despairing,
But in our lack of poignant caring —

That inmost font of ardent daring
That freely gives and offers all,
Pours out its heart past all recall
To minister unto the small —
To so indwell the mean and lowly
That they expand, unfold and slowly
Take on grandeur — altered wholly!

Move, I say! — Get out,
You beastly laziness!
What is this muddling craziness
Of simpering delay
That fills my probing conscience
With outrage and dismay!
Must I endure in me
Such lack of ardor, see
Such sluggish indecision,
– Deserving only of derision –
All lack of self-command
To do the deeds I've planned,
No fire to burn the trash of fear
And forge the dreams I hold most dear?

You luggard, inert liar,
Monster in the mire
Prone upon the dank, dark floor
Of consciousness, shut just apart
Behind my unsuspecting heart,
Will all my wrath not rouse your sleep?
Stir, stand, get going, leap
Into the sunlight — out, I say!
And labor on your knees to pay
For all your self-deceit.
There is no other way
To cure conceit.
No smallest means by which to fool
The vigilance of truth's stark school.
There is no other path to peace
Except through action's stern release.

To do one deed,
To light one spark,
To sow one seed,
To warm one heart —

To say one word
That may be heard
By heavenly ears;
To form one thought
That's forged and wrought
Of ripened tears;

To sing one song,
To live one life,
To right one wrong —
Takes homage — strife —

Takes pain and dying,
Birth and being,
Ceaseless trying,
Selfless seeing —

Takes joy and love,
Peace and sun —
The suffering of
The Risen One.

—

Blue-green and fading gold, the evening sky
Bears on its spotless breast the new born moon,
Arched like some angelic jewelled eye
That grants with silent glance a sacred boon.

FOR PERCY MACKAYE

✝

Like some swift descending Seraph
Whispering his fiery tidings
With celestial breath
    — Your face,
Pressed upon the bare, white pillow,
Caught in the instant of death;

Carved by the cadence and rhythm
Of the pulsing heart of the word
That pours in the speech which only
The ear of the spirit has heard.

Blown by the wind of the stars
Are the waves of your foam-white hair
As they flow from your high smooth brow
To be lost in the luminous air.

Moulded by mammoth will
And demon-tortured cries;
Transmuted and redeemed
By love's unfaltering eyes;

Washed and worn and welded
By the living waters of language,
That well from the womb of the world
To nourish the rivers of knowledge,

Your waxen features utter
In sounding, sculptured script
Your crowning earthly song
As a parting gift —

As hymn and offering
To those high celestial bards
Your heart-strings harked to for so long —
A paeaning of final welcome
To their swift, insweeping tidal voice
Of all-renewing calm — that choiring
Well-spring of pure world-all poetry —

The vast, encompassing,
Compassionate, awakening,
Cosmic artistry
Of heaven's sun-clad throng!

'Tis oft I feel your hand, or catch your smile,
As though you were beside me all the while,
Or suddenly look straight into your eyes
So eagerly aglow with loving speech,
Till by thus gladly gazing each in each
We can converse in quiet spirit-wise,
Aware, in inward verity of heart,
That those who meet in love death cannot part.

For P. M-K.

—

Oh, do you know what love is made of?
Have you been where it is born —
Where that frail, pierced, hand bequeaths it,
Freely, to parched pride and scorn,
To the demons who revile it —
Feeds it to the boundless pit
That gapes aghast in gorging greed
To devour it?

Have you seen in desolation
How its pure, free substance flowers,
Blooms and sheds its fairest glory
Where disaster lowers?
Wherever deepest shadows fall
Clearest light likewise is found.
Compassion is the mightier
The deadlier the ground.

Have you met its molten meaning,
Drunk its pure sun-liquid tone —
More heart-rending and more tender,
More awesome and alone,
More outpouring and forgiving,
Sovereign, upspringing
Than the full, vast voice of day —
Enfolding everything!

For deep within this planet's torture,
Torn by bloodshed, greed and strife,
There lies concealed love's lowly birthplace,
Death's entry into life —
Where, through that tiny cosmic portal,
Into each perceiving heart
Its freshening light begins to pour,
And myriad well-springs start . . . .

A spirit photosynthesis
That turns men's ailing, pale thoughts green,
And nurtures them until they open
As eyes for the unseen;
Cures, through inmost suffering,
The festering blights of greed and pride,
And when devoured by ravaging monsters,
Transforms them from inside.

Oh, if you know what love is made of,
Have been where it is born —
Been bathed and baptized in the dew
Of resurrection morn —
If you've felt the merest vestage
Of its healing and its freshness,
Have caught the slightest glimmer
Of its grace . . .

Oh, be witness to its human birth,
Its blessing on our erring race,
Anew — each instant — in your heart,
Upon this tortured earth!

"Oh, I love!"
Sang the heart.
"Love what?"
Sighed the stream
As it hardened and froze.
    "The dew on the thistle,
    The thorn on the rose,
    The gleam on the face
    Of a leaf as it grows,
    The whisper of fate
    As it eddies and flows
    Through the channels of man —
    Whither? — Love alone knows."

"Oh, I love!"
Laughed the hand.
"Love what?"
Groaned the wood
Bark-stripped and bare.
    "The feel of each form,
    Fine-chiseled with care,
    Of the unseen face
    Of all that is fair,
    The sun that is hid
    In the seed of a prayer,
    The oak springing forth
    From the soil of despair."

"Oh, I love!"
Stamped the foot.
"Love what?"
Mocked the mud
No mortal can shun.
    "The duty I do,
    The race that I run,
    The call of the road,
    The task that's begun,
    The challenge that glows
    From the goal to be won,
    The will in the selfless
    Shine of the sun."

"Oh, I love!"
  Spoke the spirit.
"Love what?"
  Scoffed the brain
In the skull where it's caught.
      "The germ that is furled
      In the shroud of a thought —
      The will that can rise
      And walk upon naught,
      Endowing with life
      The form it has wrought —
      The light which is kindled
      When dying is fraught
      With the love which through eons
      All heaven has sought."

      —

The bigness bound within me will burst me into bits.
The universe itself is knocking at my core
Like a pent-up ocean, breaking outward more and more,
Its mammoth motion mounting with every wave that hits
With head-long, tidal music upon this temporal shore,
Upon this tiny, mortal edifice of me.
Am I then but the confines of a boundless sea
That sings through all my veins a song of things to be,
Of untold treasures cast up from its cosmic lap —
Am I but bark to harbor, even as a tree,
The thundrous melodies of rising spring-tide sap:
That mighty, sweet onslaught of life that wills to pour
And press its image into myriad buds that swell,
Until the language laid within them bursts their shell
And blooms in outer eloquence of petaled speech —
The ocean's secret heart implicit within each?
Oh, shall all this ocean's life-sap ever flower thus from me,
Through opening calyxes become articulate and free,
As beauty's sun-clad orators of its unfathomed lore —
And all my countless husks at last be rent — and be no more?

Pain, that pours
In pitiless rain,
Drenching every slightest thing
In groundless gulfs of trembling gloom,
Will your endless torrents
Ever cleanse this carnate tomb?
Through your unleashed powers
Will the sunny, sure-eyed flowers
Of inward spring
Ever flourish
Once again?
Do you nourish
Secret grain?

Hush!
The ceaseless, sharp drops seem to sing;
Wait — — —
God's grace is great!
Trust —
The storms of fate.

—

When you feel you faint away,
Fall through fathoms of decay —
Hark! — and hear your Angel say:
"I am here beside you,

"With my mighty wings around you;
Feel my peace and strength surround you,
And their power will astound you.

"Look, here, straight into my gaze.
Hold fast to its loving rays —
Their light will fill you with amaze,

"And blessing will betide you
Where I guide you!"

MICHAEL

Oh, Michael, mighty quiet lord,
Michael! — fell with your swift sword
The dragon in his ebon lair
Who feeds upon my pain;
Teach me to dare,
Again and yet again,
To look him in the eye
And there descry
The cruel secret writ
With tragedy in it.

And as your sure blade flies
Straight from the sun-washed skies
Deep into his heart,
Oh, let me start
Once more upon that path
That leads through its dark door —
Right through its gaping core —
Into that star-wrought room,
Builded from the shattered tomb,
Where the gentle fires of youth
Burn upon the quiet hearth
Of truth.

Thou,
Who art the All
And core
Of me
So miserably
Lone and small;

Thou,
Who only art
The whole of every part —
Whilst I
Am naught,
Caught
In empty torment
Of dead thought.

O Thou!
Almighty breath,
Embracing all my death —
The Thee
In me,
Immaculate
And free,
That all my life
Is for —

Oh, hold me,
Fold me,
Mould me
In your mighty
Heart
Once more.

OUT THERE

Oh I have been cast away
On the tides of the dark abyss,
Swept out in the savage spray,
Sucked down in those torrent seas
That thunder, moan and hiss
Out there in the naked void,
Battering each tiniest particle
Until it is destroyed.

Out there, no mortal is spared
From gazing on the face of terror.
Out there, no mortal is spared
From looking in the eyes of error.
Out there, no mortal is spared
Utter loss —
Till each has shared
Christ's deed on the cross.

For He holds the whole chasm now deep in His heart.
He has lit it and warmed it to its farthest part.
He has gathered the tempests into His calm.
In Him no creature can come to harm.
As Son of Man, He walked on the sea.
As Son of God, He died for me.

BREATH

Silent, blessed
Peace unguessed! —
Rise and rest
At God's behest,
Tireless guest
In your human nest —
Sun-caressed,
Breath in my breast —
Healing leaven
Of limitless quest.

Wingéd bestower,
Mystery knower,
Rhythmic sower,
Wisdom-grower —
Spirit refreshed!

—

So dear
You are,
No tear
Can ever tell —
No fear
Can ever sear
Or mar
The dearness
That you are —
Your star!

So dear
Are you,
My dear!
If you but knew —
It is like silent fall
Of dew,
Drenching all
My being through —
The good
You do.

Hush! — ah hush! —
Is that the thrush
Of heaven —
The thrush
Arisen from death? —
Oh, hold your breath
And listen, listen — listen . . .

Hear,
Heart-rending, clear —
What pure tones
Gleam and glisten,
Quiver —
And like a pealing river
Pour their song
Into your heart
To burst its earthly shroud apart
And lay it wide
For that eternal, tender tide:
The hush
Of the voice
Of heaven's thrush. —

—

Overcoming, overcoming,
Day by day,
This tangled gray
Display of man-made disarray,
With over-sunning
Spirit humming! —

Ah, were I but a heavenly bee,
On Seraph wing,
Love gathering
From everything,
What honeyed human melody
I'd bring to thee!

UNUTTERED WORDS

Round about us ring
Like organ tones
Pouring from angelic throat,
Unuttered words
That fall and float
In rhythmic wonder,
Ebb and flood and swing —
Call, like cosmic thunder,
Or like the fleet,
Inestimably sweet
Choiring
Of small birds —

Words,
That peal and pour
Their mighty import,
Limpid, clear,
For all the dead to hear —
Resound,
Since time began,
From heaven's farthest shore
Down to the very floor
Of earth's utmost ground;
Through every secret chamber
Of the house of man —
And gently as a falling tear,
Beseechingly,
Knock unceasingly
Upon our deafened ear —
Begging entreatingly:
"Are there none to hear?"

It is within each other
That the answer lies . . .
'Tis there
That they are to be heard!
Every world-outpouring word!
The might
Of this frail insight,
- Its all transforming light -

Each of us who dies
Must win
Through loneliness and suffering,
As bitter and as blessed
Comforting.

For when in bleak distress
Of utter emptiness,
With silent caring
- Freed from sleep -
Gently we begin
To listen deep
Each within the other — — —
Then with patient gleaning
We learn to reap
Their selfless meaning.

When, healed of fear,
Shed of every tear,
We harken, clear,
Each within our brother
With that inward ear,
The heart,
To their archetypal art —
Steal through that lowly, crimson door,
So vast — yet infinitely small —
Across its secret sill
Of selfless will
To find there, waiting
At its inmost core,
The All —

Then, within that star-wrought hall —
Where edifice and form
Are cosmic speech,
Are destiny,
Audible to each
As inmost call
And quest —
As verity
Of all that's best
In human kind,
Expressed as path and goal
Of each striving soul,
Manifest through hand and heart and mind —

Then, at last,
Each of us may hear —
Infinitely clear,
Intimately vast —
Those sweet, unuttered words
That peal and float,
Pouring from angelic throat —
Which mould and fill
The measure of man's being
With the sounding and the seeing,
The forging and the freeing
Of their awakening will —

And each
Shall tremble there . . .
Shattered and reborn,
Heart-hallowed and heart-torn —
To catch and comprehend:
The untold tenderness,
The bleeding earnestness
Of that human inwardness,
Which is their only goal and end.

—

The voice of the world is heard
In your heart, in your head.
The surface of all that you see
Is illusion, is dead.

The language of all its beauty
Is uttered in you —
Its drama, its miraculous meaning
In the deeds that you do.

FOR ALBERT STEFFEN

✝

Quiet giant of the word,
Gentle tender of the herd,
Minstrel of the god-forsaken
Wielding cadences of light
To fashion evil into seeing,
Sculpture beauty out of night.
Toiler on the brink of being,
Moulding destiny through art, —
You show us how the dead awaken,
Till hell itself is warmed and shaken
And freedom steals into man's stricken heart.

Dramatist of cosmic deeds,
Poet of our deepest needs,
Humble friend of man and flower,
We have seen your meek strength tower
Above the onslaughts of the storm,
Lashed and lone — beheld your form,
Forged to a frail and agéd man
Flooded round with tides of youth,
Like to a gentian bathed in sun —
Yet grave as granite crags of truth
In service to a greater one . . . .
Constant to his star-wrought plan —
Guarding the chalice of hidden wine,
The sun sweet sap of the heavenly vine.

Now home, once more, your body spent,
You sup its nourishment with him,
And with untold encouragement
You smile on us from heaven's rim.

Tell me, can I die tonight
From my darkness into light?
Die but just a little way
Beyond myself into the day?
Ageless Angel who has formed me
To this fledgling, sheltered, warmed me
With your wisdom, help me now
To hatch myself — reveal me how
I can leave my littleness,
Pierce thought's thin, smooth brittleness,
Crack apart my sentient shell
That holds me in its magic spell
And clamber through my own rim out
Into the stillness all about —
Cause my selfish noise to cease
And enter your revealing peace.

—

Our eyes are the gift of the stars,
Our feet are formed by the hills
And the sod upon which they run;
Our veins are wrought by the rivers —
Our heart by the sun.

Boundless, the scope of the body —
And yet who is it that fills
This bourne of bounty — has spun
Its labyrinthian stature
And welds it to one?

Who is it really that thinks;
Who that sees and feels?
Whence is the gift of thought,
Of love that heals?

Is there then truly aught
That is our own?
No, there is naught — naught —
Save You alone.

For all the years we've been together
Through sunshine, wind and stormy weather,

For all the days that we have spent
Whereby our questing souls have blent,

For all the moments we have risen
Above our own small earthly prison

To see within each other's face
A countenance of heavenly grace, —

For all your patience, dearest one,
Like rays of mellow, healing sun,

For every struggle and each storm
Through which we've wrought each other's form,

And for your love — like secret dew
That makes life's wilting meadow new,

Take this rose!
It is my heart —
For you
It grows.

—

Golden leaves against the blue —
A holy, secret rendezvous.

Choral trees, caressed by sky —
As uttered poetry we die.

Confiding love — pure speech of gold.
Unuttered peace — bright breath of blue.

One cup of brimming sun we hold,
Earth and heaven, I and you.

All-seeing,

    The beings of heaven behold you.

All-feeling,

    The fingers of destiny mould you.

All-bearing,

    The creatures of nature uphold you.

All-caring,

    The arms of the Saviour enfold you.

—

THE GIFT
AND THE GIVER

Everything I see
You reveal to me.

Every truth I know
You have made to grow.

Each hope and each feeling —
Your gift and your healing.

And all that I do
Is for You.

Life-infused, light-imbued world,
So breathlessly intimate, awesome —
I love you so dearly!
I did not know you had held me for infinite ages
So inexpressibly nearly.
Only the anguish at imminent loss of you told me
So inconceivably clearly —
Clad in your limitless selflessness, silence and mercy,
Christ — 'tis You really! —

—

As the bare and barren rock
Cups the virgin water,
Clear, as when a lifeless hand
Lovingly has caught her,
So the rock of intellect
In its barren palm
Cups a tiny sparkling spring,
Bubbling cool and calm —
Freedom's clear, refreshing font
Welling from death's sill,
With all heaven mirrored deep
In its limpid will, —
Ever self-replenishing,
If we will but drink
From the quiet, crystal pool
That gushes when we think.

FOR RUDOLF STEINER

How can we ever learn to fathom
The awesome deed that you achieved,
Or ever learn how to give thanks
For the boon we have received.

For you unlocked the shrine of heaven,
That darkness had sealed hard and fast;
Reclaimed the sacred, triune key
From out the depths where it was cast.

And now the door stands open wide
For all mankind to make their way;
And both wide worlds of earth and spirit
Are flooded in the clear new day.

From the heights and the depths and the encircling spheres,
You then crafted, as master, a world work of art —
The new temple of mankind, arisen through fire,
And layed it as a Grail-gift in each out-reaching heart.

For the love of mankind you laid down your life
To lay open cosmic-sun-thought to the whole light-starved earth.
The Word of the World rang out through your voice
To illumine man's pathway through death and rebirth.

No longer can dire hordes enslave men through darkness
In such clear out-flooding of resurrection's light,
For those they hold captive in death-bound blindness
Can awake now, sun-quickened, to free spirit-sight.

Oh how, our hearts ask, are we ever to thank you! . . .
Yet, as true thanks ever blooms new through every birth plight,
Let us bear a free-sun-deed each day into life,
With the whole of our heart, of our mind and our might.

A sun-deed to harbor the Light of the World,
Who filled the Grail-cup from the sun-fonts above;
A free-deed to give answer from the deeps here beneath,
With the human sun-streamlet of our outpouring love.

Clear eye, dear eye,
Filled with the sun,
Vessel where earth
And heaven are one.

Blue eye, true eye,
Flower and star,
Chalice where love
And wonder are.

Eye of the infinite, eye of man!
Who is it wakens you,
Orb of the All —
In the depth, in the height,
Who kindles your sight?

Only He can
Whose voice is the light!

For K.E.

—

With unending patience, glorious strength
And whimsical mirth,
You plant here small deeds, selfless seeds,
In the waiting earth
For future sun-birth as cosmic grain
– Fruit of long pain and humble dearth –

Till, ripened above,
They shall fall again as fresh star-rain
For the blessing of men —
Clear, death-redeeming life-drops of love,
Bequeathing to all the infinite worth,
Mute dignity, nobility
And deep humility
Of pure humanity!

That humorous, dry, lovingly shy,
Encumbered mystery
Of unobstructed, high
Individuality.

For R.K.M.

Oh, how many times,
Great Artist and Master,
Must I be made over,
Made molten and bent
To your ageless designing,
Be melted and tested
And tried in your fire,
Till you are at last
Content —

Be beaten and battered,
Hammered and wrought
In the intricate welding
Of substance and thought —

Be fashioned and moulded
And thrust in the flame —
Every time altered,
Yet ever the same.

You view me now newly
And test me once more,
Forever in quest
Of that exquisite ore

So strong and so faultless,
So supple, so pure,
That beset by all evil
It still will endure.

Oh, how many times
Great Artist and Master
Of the heavenly forges
Of replenishing flame —
White-hot with will-kindled,
Sun-molten thought —
Shall I be retried
In the infinite fires
Of your cosmic conceiving,
Till the metal of man
Has been wrought!

'TWAS THERE

'Twas at the turn of the road,
Which is called the Way of Becoming,
That the monster was lying in wait,
Where, just as the sun peered up,
He lept from his lair —
And, caught unaware,
I lay wounded and lashed,
Spewed with his venom of hate, gnashed
By the furious fangs
Of the thirsting, three-headed monster:

That prowler who preys on the sweet, rich sap
That sings and flows
In the teeming streams of the tree of life —
Pulses and grows
In the ripening strivings
And ardors of those
Who pursue the road
To fulfillment,
Across that vast valley of conflict,
No traveler yet has escaped.

And there, as I lay,
And saw on the ground
The seeping blood of my heart,
That ran from the rent
His ravaging forceps had torn;
Saw all of the burgeoning portent,
It had succored and builded, borne
Away, in a torrent of pain —
Its deep red stream now steeped in bane,
In the first glad beams of the dawn —

There, in its gleam,
More clear than dream,
Out of the sun there stepped a form,
More free than air —
Than aught, more fair — —
'Twas there
That He came to me
Again
And gathered the blood in His own cupped hands —
Held it warm — held it long
And tenderly,
Reached it close that I might see
Its quiet light —
Then, clear and bright as crimson dew —
Gave it to me —
Anew.

'Twas there that He bent
And closed the rent
And lifted me from the ground —
And at His smile,
As He helped me rise,
Day — engulfed the skies.

The earth lies scarcely breathing
In the stillness now of evening
Like a wondering maiden, innocent and blessed,
And gives a sigh of deep contentment
As she lays herself to rest.
Upon her breast,
The little calves are gambling
Out across the wide soft-shadowed meadows,
While the ponderous cows,
Raising their heads to gaze,
Stoop once more to graze
In long-earned unconcern
Of motherly content.
The day is spent.
The moon has risen in the east and in the west
The sun goes down.
A lingering glory of expectant peace
Broods above the valley's rhythmic form
As twilight comes,
Laiden with the soft, spiced fragrance
Of autumnal rest.

And we, illustrious mortals!
Could we but be, consciously,
Even in small degree,
As quiet —
With all creation
So at one! —
Meet, with such confident acceptance
The approaching dark;
Feed, with such unwavering devotion
Upon those fields of fresh, illimitable calm
Which nourish with their timeless verdure —
Unheeded and unguessed —
Our warring world. . . .
And with the dawn,
Utterly refreshed,
Greet, as those new born,
The never failing sun.

There is a valley that we love —
A melody of hills and fields,
With brook below and sky above,
Steeped in peace the sunlight yields.

There is a house above the road
With nesting robins by the door.
No dearer, lovelier abode
Was known to any man before.

Between the rocks upon the slope,
What glory springs out of the soil
To fill our hearts with joy and hope
In such abundance for our toil.

Your tiny shack beneath the trees —
A haven of hushed weathered wood
That opens on the mysteries
Where you have searched and understood.

Ah, truly 'tis so blessed a place,
This valley, garden, porch — our home! —
'Twill shelter you in all its grace
No matter where you roam.

For K.E.   May 7, 1964

—

Blue sky, blue sky!
Mute gaze of immaculate being;
    Clear sky, dear sky!
Wake us with the quick of your seeing;

    New earth, true earth!
Young sun in the dark of the sod;
    Bright earth, light earth!
The home of the death-risen God;

    Bless us, caress us
With breath of your infinite spring;
    Think us and link us
With the sweet core of each living thing.

For K.E.   May 7, 1971

FOR KARL EGE
1973
✝

Can I be still enough to hear,
Within the mighty silence
Where you are —
So intimately near
And yet so infinitely far —
The inmost meaning
Of what your being
Speaks to me,
And dry away the tear
That blinds my eye,
Cleansing it to see
In ever surer, purer contours,
Impassionately clear,
The stature of your ageless self. —

Oh, quivering heart,
Focus of heaven and earth,
Storm-swept, sun-fed, seed-bed of us both,
Cupped in Christ's quickening keep,
May I be
Still enough — wake enough
To meet
Your constant, star-lit gaze,
And in the glad embrace
Of its transmuting rays,
To tend
Your spaceless need, —
Mend
Each frayed and broken end
Of destiny —

Greet,
Perceive
And overflowingly receive
At last
Your instant, breathing,
Clear indwelling entity of being —
Unwaveringly true
In quality, in texture and in hue,
And in the grace
Of inmost speech:

The secret sum and nature
Of the one
Who wore the form I loved,
Inhabited and built
The hand-hewn, star-strewn
Mystery
I knew
As you.

—

The peace that lay in breathless death
Upon your finely moulded features,
Like a star-reflecting sea,
The harmonies of destiny,
The sun-tuned strength,
The beauty of divine expectancy
That hovered like a sheen of grace
About the contours of your upturned face,
Their bold-hewn patterns sculptured
By the power of truth
To the purity of youth —

The eager gaze of your closed eyes
Aloft into a land of flooding light,
The smile that touched your parted lips
As though your Angel had just come
And reached his hand to welcome you —

The courage and the calm that rang,
The life which sprang
About your fragile frame
At his clear, heavenly call —
And as the All in you awoke . . .
The sun-lit word
Your freeing being spoke. —

This human script —
Core and image of your spirit worth —
Is graven for eternity
Upon my heart.
Oh, would that all the world might likewise see
And read
This parting gift
You wrote into the earth!

Yes, you have traveled that sunward path
Where wonder and will are woven and wed
With the light of thought with which life is fed.
Steadfast, unswerving, faithfully serving
The heavenly art of human learning,
You have followed its stern, exacting course
To its quickening source.

Through achievement, adversity, pain and song,
Failure and fortitude, blessing and wrong,
Defender of truth and befriender of youth,
By starlight, by day,
You have walked its full length
With all of your strength,
Every step of the way —

Forming with vigor at each footfall
A powerful image inwrought with all
That builds and moulds, since time began,
The living creative substance of man —
Love that warms, heals and transforms,
Truth which sets free,
Awakened spirit, gifted to see,
Forging anew the life to be —

Where at the last, from final loss,
Out of your waking, breathless heart,
Breaking the frost of death apart,
Roses bloom from earth's dark cross,
Each crimson chalice reaching wide
To catch the resurrection's tide;
And as you breathe its fullness there,
Freshening peace floods everywhere.

Yes, you have trod
That silent path of sun and sod
And stepped with wakeful seeing
Through death as spirit being
Into the brimming, boundless heart
Of the Risen One,
To join there the chorus of the helpers of men
And gather new forces to return again.

So suddenly you went
To join the living dead,
While there was still so much unsaid,
So many hopes unsolved,
Such human store unspent,
That the gaping rent
Your leaving left within my heart
Has torn the kernel of my self apart
And laid it open to the quick —
Bared, down to its quivering core:
The hidden fibers and the bleeding flesh
Of those soul substances which weave
The whole great, pulsing mortal mesh
Of our immortal destiny,
All wounded, raw —

Yet there,
At the very quick of such despair,
With piercing certainty, I see,
Heart-rendingly,
How, through the anguish of the wound,
Its all-engulfing pain —
Like the swift, fusing mystery of flame
Lifting from the crumbling ash
In clarifying light —
By such burning change, we wake
To glimpse — and then partake
Of a love more free, more clear,
More near, revealing, dear —
Deepening more
And ever more. . .
Than on the earth
We could have known
Before.

Come!
Dear one, who wakes over yonder,
   I will sing you a song: —
Through my eyes, through my heart,
Look at our garden
And see there
   The joy of the opening flowers
   You have loved for so long;

Hear there, within *me*,
   The breathing tones of their colors,
   The weaving harmonies
      Of the lilies, the roses, the phlox,
      Bright black-eyed susans and spires of yuka
         Chiming with lupins and purple bells —
            The high sigh of the trees,
            The base notes of the rocks;

All of the rhythmical wonder
Played by star-fingered beings
   On the strings of the light and the air,
   On the trumpets, the pipes and the drums
      Of wind and water and earth,
   Like a swarm of cosmic bees
      Bringing this singing hive
      Of beauty and life to birth
         From the dearth
         Of winter;

Vanquishing there, with intricate delight,
   The somber might
   Of snow and ice
      To strangle and harden
      All delicate contours of hope —
   And with infinite pardon,
      For the stubbornness of their thorny, hoary,
      Arrogant denial
         Of love's sure faith
         In each new trial,

They now burst here once more into bloom,
  Greeting the day
In this sun-bathed, heaven-revealing disarray —
  The miracle and glory,
  The mysterious story,
  Of our dear rambling,
    Clambering
    Garden.

Yet while you behold this song
  Through me,
You are now there within and behind it,
  No longer outside, as once,
    Seeking to find it, as I —
  But a singing part of those beings,
    Who, in the infinite flowing
    Of their shaping and growing,
      Know how and know why
      We live and we die —

Are one with the song itself —
  And now sing it in me,
    Spirit-awakeningly —
      There
    Where the world is fed
    And life is led
      In the intimate detection
      Of the resurrection.

Ah, how sweet the garden smells
As so it sings and tells: —
  Through all that you perceive through me
  And I receive through you,
    Through all we do
    Together, in such wise,
    We work upon the gleaming key
      To unlock the mystery
      Of paradise.

The sorrow is so great
Each morning when I wake,
It seems as though my heart
Would break apart,
My being burst asunder,
With the echoes of the rending grandeur
Of the heavenly drama
Being now enacted,
Where you are newly born,
Just under
The fragile veil
Of our unwitting slumber.

Like the chastening flash
And impact of starry lightning,
Speaking with the pealing voice
And cleansing clash
Of cosmic thunder,
Its echoes roll
Beneath the brittle surface
Of our blatant everyday —

Leaving,
In the pent stillness of their wake,
Like potent balm
In the vast gulf of grief,
A breath of fresh inpouring wonder,
A swift intake
Of pure rejuvenating air —
Hushed anticipation,
Glistening, listening,
Gleaming,
In the newness —
Everywhere.

No, I am not alone,
For you are always near
Where I need only to call you —
To bring you something worthy
To focus your attention upon —
And then you are here —

Love, to warm you,
Quiet, to hear you,
Hope, to pierce
        The shadows which hide you
        There, where the beings of heaven
        Betide you.
Truth, to see you,
Patience, to reach you,
Peace, to free you
        To follow the path to the sun,
        Where the clothing you newly will wear
        Shall be woven and spun.
Trust, in the outstretched hand of Christ
        To guide you —
        And to wing my feet to walk
        Beside you.

                    —

See, the hawthorn blooms
Beside your dear shack door,
Speaking forever more
The language of your passing —
And yet the hope its crimson holds in store,
That is just starting to restore
To budding life the ravages of winter
And to pour
Its fragrant wonder on the waiting air,
Tells now in rending melody quite new
What all its bloom is for:
To bring to you
In each outreaching, heart-red petal-cup
My inmost prayer —
Love's brimming spirit-fare —
Glistening there
For you to drink its living sun-light up.

This wound —
The tender, open entryway
Through death,
Can never heal —
And yet its constant presence
Can reveal
What death is for . . . .
And this is more,
Much more.

—

Let no one think he is not guilty;
For the sluggish streams of wrong
Wind and creep,
Run, more dark and deep
Than gaping cosmic night,
Seep, through all the potent star-wrought soil
Of striving human kind —
And each must weep.

Yet, let no one think he is not innocent.
For the quenchless springs of chastity
Well, more clear,
More merciful and dear,
Than morning's freshening light,
And steal through all the barren lands laid waste
By mortal hand and mind —
So none need fear.

For the waters of our tears
Become the hidden fonts of hope.
The limpid bounty of our higher source
Hides in the fertile womb of death
Purifying man and earth
With spirit birth.

Now that you are free
Of earth's infirmity,
How active, yonder, you must be!
How eager, awed, absorbed, intent —
All your fervent being bent
On offering the glowing fruits you've grown,
The heart-ripe harvest of all you've done and known
In ardent toil upon the treasure-soil of years,
To the star-eyed beings whom you meet,
Those far-eyed guardians you so gladly greet
In the streaming life of the encircling spheres —

Holding there deep converse
With angelic hosts on high,
Listening to music welling
From the vast bosom of the sky,
Learning those fine hymnic laws
That underlie the cosmic scores
Used in this orchestral school,
Whereby to forge and ply
The fair creation of the new —

The mighty transformations
Of world-storm-clouds into dew,
The secrets of the crown of thorns
And of the roses' crimson hue —
The grammar, source and inmost glory
Of man's eternal, archetypal story
Uttered in the molten language of the true.

Oh, on this wonder-pathway
May
The Holy Trinity light through
And shelter
You.

FOR FLINKA

The devotion of a dog to man,
The selfless entry of its soul
Into the heart, the mind,
The humblest habits and details of humankind,
Put all our learned pride and pettiness to shame.

Regardless of our thought, or deed,
For good or ill,
This same infallible fidelity
Remains unchanged,
A mystery of constancy
That at some future day,
In the great course of all-requiting destiny,
We still must win the power to repay.

Of such a mystery was Flinka wrought
And all the language of affection
That she brought:
The beauty of her sleek, black form,
Her slender, sinewed legs,
Her long expressive tail
And noble, alert head;
The humble well-springs of her golden eyes —
Now sovereign calm,
Now spirited expectance, all aware —
Her lifted ears
Tuned to the distant air.

And oh, the speed and joy with which she sped
Across the rhythmic reaches of the valley
Toward the far off veils of blue —
Out to the very borders of the sky
And back — to frolic in the drifting leaves,
As leaping high
She skillfully retrieves
The flying stick her joyful master threw.

No wind, nor wingéd angel was more swift —
More fleet —
Only at night to lie,
In utter homage
To the ritual of all our human lore of life,
There on the carpet at our feet.

Or, as so oft before,
When we had been away
All day —
The instant knocking of her tail upon the floor
As we unlocked the door. —
Yet savage and commanding
Were her teeth and bark
In passionate protection
Of her Mortal in the dark.

And at the last,
When years had passed,
With what high, patient dignity
She bore her suffering,
The fading now of all her body's wonder-web
Of joy and strength —
Going to her end
With a meek majesty
And unwavering trust,
As only the mute grandeur of a higher being's
Benign bounty can expend.

So noble, fleet, affectionate and good
A creature of this earth
Was she!
Oh, may her name and worth,
The blessing that she brought
To her master and to me,
That brims my heart
With a hymn of human gratitude,
Ring out in light, like a bright star,
In homage to her spirit-archetype,
Out there within the zodiac,
Where the group-souls of all the varied animals
Of God's creation
Are! —

IN DEFENSE OF THE WORD

Oh, fie on you who foul the word!
And tear its rhythmic life to tatters,
Who seal its hymnic soul
In single-letter prison-cells,
Then shamelessly proceed to splice
Its slaughtered parts with media glue
In advertisement's strangling vice,
All cleanly clamped, assembled and compounded
By Mammon's syndicated pressure pumps,
And intergeared, on sponsor-wheels,
With endless reels
Of those reiterantly daft
Jet-journalism auguries and spoils
Of super-sin
In tinsel-foils,
Gleaned from the halls of government and graft,
From science lobbies and the filthy fray
Of man and atom disarray —
Whereby you fashion, fuse and form
A diabolical, computered manikin
Who struts and shouts and clatters,
Declaiming, a multi-billion-fold —
In monitored, cacophonous cries
Across the continents —
His tragic dirge
Of ravaged, drivelling rhetoric,
Homogenized
With erudite inanities. . . .
A monstrous brew
Inflicted on mankind,
Avidly distilled
From greed, soul-muck and lies.

Only each conscious, living word,
Tended and grown in inner sun,
To flower as insight's opening eye:
Perceiving why
All must die
To live —
And spoken by
The brimming, world-embracing heart of man
Upon the full breath-stream of cosmic calm,

As utterance of spirit birth on earth,
Can heal the harm —
And give to all, through each,
That truth-imbuing, trust-renewing,
Error-righting, soul-uniting,
All delighting
Virgin voice of human worth —
The freedom-reaping balm
Of speech.

—

REACH ME YOUR HAND!

Dear one,
On your path to the sun —
So soon I shall join you.
When my work is done,
Reach me your hand
On the rays of your star
From the living land
Of light
Where you are,
And hold mine fast,
Until at last
I greet you there
On the golden stair
Where we climb,
To the sound of heaven's chime,
Toward the radiant Being
Of Healing —

The eternal transformation,
Creation and adoration
Of the fair, the good and the true,
That feeds the fonts of the free
And quickens the quick of the new —
Till all of mankind at length may find
That holiest goal of each human soul:
To be blessed to see
Love's matchless face —
Glimpse —
Its all-revealing mystery
And grace.

SUCH ALONE IS PRACTICAL

Oh, for some human soul today
Who can be practical!
For someone who
Can do
The lowly, holy deeds of life
In living consort with the cosmos and the earth;
Who knows the worth
Of caring —
The melody of sharing —
Knows the free, benign necessity
Of beauty,
Which turns all bitterness of duty
Into honey-hives of healing benison —
And can infuse all these as one
Into the art of hand and foot and tongue.

Someone who can look, imagine and see through,
Design, and then with courage and dexterity can do
What life's events demand
With such selfless, glad command
That he serves both God and man;
For such meek structural material
To build humanity a home
Alone is practical
And will withstand,
In substance and in form,
The coming storm.

Those who practice the conceits
Of calculation and deduction,
Applying parasitic rules,
And madly chase the neutrons and the molecules
With mind computers,
All in praise of practicality,
Only succeed in littering the earth
With glittering swarms of gadget-lice,
- Each creature worth a fortune, offered at half price -
With non-degradable, demonic beasts of burden
Let loose in endless herds of streamlined, polished grime
- All guaranteed to increase time -

A whole new breed of dead, computered phantom facts
- Free, world wide, without a tax -
Innoculated for each life-disease, to feed
The human mind:

Wraiths, who slyly suck the substance of men's souls
For their own sustenance,
And gloat upon the greed
Their thriving corpses fester
In the body social of mankind.

Or those, again, who gather, amid ardor and derision,
The faded legacies of ancient vision —
Subtly mixed and brewed
Into sedacious potions for the ailing multitude
To restore the vanished eyesight of the blind.

While all the venom spewed
From Mammon's giant factories of fission-fusion
- Those deadly storage-tanks of total devastation -
Causes the poison-ravaged earth
To cry aloud in mounting tremors of deep cosmic grief
Lest she become so crippled, martyred and maligned
That she be forced to forfeit and forego
Her holy office to bestow,
On all who cling unceasingly to her great girth
The life-endowing bounty of the mysteries of birth.

Is this to be the end, then,
To man's practicality?
Or can he still awake
To deal with this intolerable state
Before it is too late? —

Open wide his sense-embattled and encrusted eyes to see
That when the means are foul, so will the end be, too —
See, that it's the death-clot deep in his own thinking
That is the festering source
Which leads on this annihilation-course:
The paralyzing greed of each matter-bated, cancer-weighted concept,
Purged of every vestage of divine respect. —

Whereas, within the very quality and core
Of the heart's meek, rhythmic artistry, its selfless lore,
The means are clean, their out-put pure and true.

If then such fine heart-artistry be ministered to thought,
Be interfused within its lethal, abstract entities
To quicken in those clogged-up streams, till it ignite
Their inert substance; cause it to ray forth and glow
With fresh, warm, sun-born light —
Light, that is the focal property
Of that life-perceiving, form-conceiving faculty of sight
- Kindling quickener of all darkness that has died -
Which can refashion and redeem the erring currents of the will —
Then this could be the cure,
And is the pure
Creation-font of every wholesome deed that man can do.

For the methods of true art are never tactical.
The ends which they achieve accrue
From patient practice, yet are ever new.
They are enactable
Without release of devastation, of pollution, or privation,
For they revere the laws of life that are arisen from death,
Use the transubstantiating rhythms of the heart and breath,
Employ perception that engages with the actual.
Their very nature is the more fulfilled
The more finely they can serve and build
What through spirit is revealed and by the heart is willed —
And such alone is practical!

—

Alas!
The countenance of man is ever rarer
On this earth,
Which is infested with a hybrid race —
Inhabited by semi-pseudo beings who disgrace
Their human worth.

And yet! —
The countenance of man is ever fairer
For this earth,
And startles us with ever keener grace
When rarely it is seen. — For every feature bears the trace
Of spirit birth!

FOR CHRISTY

For all the blessings you are ever bringing,
For all the gladness round about you springing,
From far and wide a melody is winging,
Through earth and air a rhyme of joy is ringing,
In all our hearts a song of thanks is singing:

Oh, may the Holy Spirit's light betide you,
May Michael with his angels ever guide you,
The kings and shepherds hasten close beside you,
The heaven's quickening speech confide in you,
For the Word is risen — and will abide with you!

—

O you — who are yonder!
Your silent help
Seeps unseen
Into our daily deeds —
Bathing all our needs
In cosmic dew,
Let fall by you;

Or springs between
Our barren thoughts,
Like starry flocks
Of mountain flowers, clustered
In the crevices of rocks,
Causing our sterile world to wax and bloom
With those unnumbered, unexpected wonders
Which transform the gloom
Of this impending doom
That grips our modern life
In global strife, —

Strewing our iniquity
With the verdant freshness of fidelity,
Our stoney blindness
With the countless flowering eyes of kindness,
Our erring ways —
With heaven's gaze.

All of our striving,
All that was done! —
Who will remember
The labors begun,
Those well accomplished
And those still undone?

Who will remember
Here on the earth?
Will any remember
On this side of birth?

Yet on yon side of death
They see and recall —
Those without breath,
They experience all
That was done here together
In willing and thought,
That we wrestled to realize —
All that was wrought
Of the heart's deepest yearnings,
The goals that were sought. . . .
While hierarchical beings
Work deep in this web,
This vast human fabric —
In its flow and its ebb.

For the Cherubim stride
In the midst of our deeds
Sowing and reaping
Apocalyptical seeds.
While the Seraphim nurture
The humming sun-sea
That warms and ripens
World destiny —
That heart-enkindling
Mystery
That echoes and seeks,
Transforms and speaks
In you and in me.

THE SUN-LIT ART OF THE HUMAN HEART

Oh, why is it
That almost everybody is afraid today
To speak out of his heart! —
But thinks that everything he has to say
Must be concise, clipped, clever and self-satisfied!
Must have appeal — oh yes! — and be at any rate undignified,
Crooned, perhaps — in some appalling, deadly way —
Or just straight modern jargon, drab and gray.

Is it their fear of ridicule?
Their horror to be thought a fool? —
Fleeing the sentimental — to at least keep cool! —
Or are they the unwitting tool
Of hidden motives,
Harbored in secreted, semi-conscious creatures
Who infest men's souls
And carry out their avid votives
To Mammon, on the altars
Of his vicious goals?

And to what end?
Whither do they lead us?
What do they portend?

Without the heart — all mankind would be bled and blind;
All inner human contact undermined;
Each sealed in isolation in his frozen cell —
A lonely hell! —

Without the heart — the human mind
Would atrophy and turn to mental-stone,
Its powers operated for utility alone,
Geared and sized to spy-out and apply,
To covet, trap and kill! —

Without the heart — the will
Would rage in dark, obscene brutality,
Fester to gigantic world catastrophy —
Only to plunge into a sea of impotence,
Reduced, by its own excess and rank futility,
To nil! —

Man would be destroyed —
An empty flask
For Mammon's evil wine to fill!

'Tis only when at length all three,
The heart, the mind, the will
Can live and work in harmony,
That this travesty,
This brutal storm of enmity,
Will at last be still!

And of the three —
As Mammon knows! —
It is the heart
That holds out to the others
A slender, gleaming key
To set them free! —

It is the golden mystery
Of art! —
That faculty which shields, transforms
And heals its stricken brothers;
Takes them by the hand and leads them to consort
In loving alchemy, —
That free, divine activity of man
Which foils, with beauty's brimming mastery,
The shameful aims of evil's monstrous plan.

Oh, decide! Make haste and act! — The hour is already late! —
The storm-clouds of the world-all lower wild! — Near or far —
No matter where, or what, or who you are. —
Pause! — Take breath! — And let us start
To speak, to think and to create —
With full courage and full weight —
Out of the wonder, warmth and truth,
The wisdom, power and eternal youth,
Of that tempest-torn,
Love-flooded, love-upborne,
Sun-lit art
Of the human heart! —

—

THE VOICE
OF AWAKENING MAN

THEE

I

Who am I in me
Am an eye
With which to see
The wonder
That is me,

Not I
But Thee,
Thou I
From on high
Who am I
Who see,
And thereby
I
Who am free.

Thou wonder,
Over and under,
Hid in my heart
Who art
Me.

Dear thoughts
Who light my way
With unseen ray
More radiant than day! —

When you lay
Parched and gray,
I did not know
Each inmost core
- If warmed and listened for -
Could grow within life's womb
To leaf and bloom:
   A living, giving,
   Light-outpouring,
   Spirit-storing
      Star —
The flowered seeing
Of an angel being!

Conceived, as heaven's deeds,
Sun-grown afar,
And cast from cosmic floor —
A myriad spirit seeds,
Each potent with the bright,
Heart-wakening star-lore
Of angel-sight —
Your shadowy husks are rife
With Michaelian life,
Potentized in the perfection
Of the resurrection
   To quicken infinite
   Croplands of light
   On earth,
   For man's rebirth!

And yet we still
Incarcerate your corpses
In the brain
And do not heed
Your spirit-risen might!

Dear thoughts! —
I did not know before
How merciful and fair
     You are!

Yes — the heart
Can think,
Not just the brittle brain.
The heart can think
With pure sun-art
Aglow —
And its crimson flow
Of warm upwelling,
Death-dispelling
Thought,
Caught
Within the selfless, star-inwrought
Vessel of the human mind
- A radiant pool of resurrecting light -

There, within that crystal cup,
Immaculately offers up
Its quenchless draught
Of life
To thirsting man,
To rescue him from parched starvation,
Where he reels upon the crumbling brink
Of self-annihilation —

Swept ever onward by the rage
Of the whirlwinds of world strife
That wage
Their siege of inhuman enslavement
With tidal vortexes of shattered facts,
Computer-manned
And Mammon-radar-interwrought,
By remote command
From the innermost caverns
Of material naught.

For it is the innocent, dauntless art
Of this living, spirit libation
To link
Each parted particle,
Each hungering heart,
Into the whole,

To wake, unburden and redeem
Each squandered soul —

When, cupped within the quiet of the mind,
The sun within the heart
Begins at last to think —
Like the awesome sound of far-off rousing thunder
Proclaiming the approaching dawn
Of the age of apocalyptic wonder,
When its benign, out-beaming bounty
Shall heal the hungry, halt and blind
Of all human kind.

—

Purged in the faultless fires of courage
To the quickening ore of peace,
The mighty trials borne
And transformed by your soul
Lie furled within the Word —
And at the touch of spring,
Like to a deep-eyed gentian
Brimmed with heaven's gold,
    Hold,
  As in its opening bowl,
  The all-awakening sun.

For G. d.R.

—

Death and birth
Create and devastate the earth.
Birth and death
Give both soul and spirit breath.
And yet the will of neither one
Could be constrained, or could be done —
Whereby the humble, fertile seed
Of freedom can become a deed —
Without the loving Risen Sun.
For life is dying into death.
Death arising into life.
And in between, the human heart,
That bleeds for both in moral strife
To hold and harmonize the two,
Receives the sustenance of art —
The secret — ever forged anew.

O Holy Spirit!
At last I have found you,
Have heard your voice
In the silence around you,
Have caught your gaze
Through the thorns that have crowned you,
Have supped from the cup
Of the death which surrounds you,
As the night cups the light
Of the morning star.

You who are
The font and the form,
The immaculate hue
And utterance of heaven's sight,
Unleashing, through wounds of freedom's light,
The cosmic well-springs of the true —
Belovéd creator and tender
Of the eternally new,
Who wakes on the breast of the One
Whose heart is the sun.

—

Oh, words are the eyes
    Of hierarchical beings,
Organs wrought
    For invisible seeings.

And rhythm is born
    Of the wheeling and wreathing,
The eternal heaving
    Of the stars' vast breathing.

And what then are rhymes
    But the answering chimes
For the wedding of deeds
    To bring forth fresh seeds.

For a poem is man
    And woman in one,
The earth and the firmament,
    Stars — and the sun!

Ah, what deeds
Are waiting to be done.
Yonder — up above —
Where the seeds
We sowed on earth
Will be sprouting in the sun,

Where the thoughts we brought alive here
Will become a honey-hive there
To feed us for the task
Of love
The angels ask
Of us,
As they speed us on our way
Into heaven's day,
That thus,
As pupils in their school we may
Learn to fathom what they say —

To remodel and remake,
Refashion each mistake,
Create new star-wrought patterns
Of destiny,
New singing faculties
Of sun-fraught wonder,
To bring again to men in earth-life
Here down under —

New dramas and new symphonies
Of cosmic- and of human-kind,
New mysteries,
To wake the slumberers
And heal the halt and blind —

All done alone by grace and virtue
Of the power and the speech
The Holy Spirit opens
And offers unto each.

How often — I have had to walk
          Upon the sea,
With this unfathomable pain of sinking
          Sweeping over me —
The strength, with which we daily swim
          Our earthly way,
All spent — and gone — —
And yet, there is no ground to tread upon!
          No help! — except to stand
                    And walk —
          Walk upright on the sea . . .
          Firmly, trustingly —
And reaching touch the untold mercy
          Of Your guiding hand
                    Upholding me.

—

Dear, vast, celestial hosts,
Intelligences of divine degree,
Artisan of pure reality,
Who built my frame,
Who tend my organs
And ignite my inmost flame —

In awed awareness
Of your majesty,
Your rhythmic clarity
And peace,
May my ability
To serve the matchless mystery
Of your creative ends —

Nourished, schooled and disciplined,
Through daily deeper veneration
For your cosmic art
Of in- and ex-carnation —
Ever gratefully
Increase.

Oh, how constantly,
So it seems, today,
Everybody turns their backs on You
And walks away,
Or, hurriedly just passes by
Without a glance,
Never pausing, quietly,
To see
Who watches silently
And waits —

Who it may be?
Who is this never-failing friend,
Patient beyond end,
Ever there,
So innocent and fair,
Yet awesome, vast,
Beyond all grasp! —

How many never even think
To speak
A gentle, searching word
To You,
To ask
Your need and task,
Or even just to know
Whether You might be
But fantasy,
Or indeed are true!

Still — there are a few —
And oh, so many more,
Assuredly,
Than can be guessed —
Who do
Pause —
And speak with You.

COME!

Barbarism looms on every side,
Threatening to swallow up mankind.
The gluttonous jaws of greed are gaping wide;
While demons, crouched in intricate machines,
Devour man's soul and automate his mind,
Proving, through death's deceit, that cells and genes
And warring neutrons are his sole creators,
That these contrive to build the universe
By chance, and thus become the perpetrators
Of our sins and passions — the luck, or curse,
Which nothing can escape. — Why worry, then,
About the lofty goals of mice and men! —

Oh, can we not awake to flay such nonsense!
Is there no recourse to sound reason, no defense,
No weapon capable of bold redress?
Yes — yes! — There is a cure. — Oh yes!
There is a healing for everyone who tries
To pull the wool from his own spirit eyes:

Perceive and use the spirit's light in thought;
Receive and give the spirit's warmth in love;
Revere and tend the spirit's might in action;
In the living presence of the resurrection. —
'Tis by these means that man awakens from above.
By these means his weapons of defense are wrought.
By these means he finds himself as man,
Sprung of a celestial artist's master-plan:
The uttered mystery of love — set free . . .
'Tis thus it can be heard in you and me.

Oh, take heart! — Begin! — Do not delay,
Pause, or falter, in the deadly fray;
But, armed with rays of heart-sharp spirit-sight,
Dare to rescue mankind from its plight. —
See! Their light now riddles evil with dismay.
Stabbed by love's pure beams, it quails in fright —
Its hideous hopes lit-through! — it flees away. . . .

Come! — The great Archangel leads the way
Through all the storms of outrage and decay,
Of tidal conflict, torn by hatred, scorn
And envy — on into the far-flung dawn
That ushers in the Spirit's cleansing day —
When, by the courage each shall thus display,
All men with sun-lit organs shall be born!

A POETIC OVERTURE
In Prelude to the Coming Age

With Festival Choruses in Seven Parts

—

SILENT CHORUS
Of Those Who Hunger and Thirst

On the quest for the goal of man,
Where the awesome eyes of conscience,
Unclosing, gaze and glow,

Light-hungering souls of the homeless,
Who are becoming a chorus of more —
Pierced to our innermost core,
Where life itself is hushed,
Torn, in the tidal strife of mankind,
Anguished, by the desolate plight of the blind,
Heart-tried
Lest truth remain denied —
Mute — we entreat
And in silence pray
To the spirit who wakes in man to speak
What the living spirit alone can say —
   For who other is able to utter
   What only the freshets of silence
   Are gifted to voice and avow:

How,
In hunger and thirst,
In a waste-land accursed. . . .
There — enkindling the uttermost void,
Like the untold refreshment of day
Overflooding the valley of loss
With the dawn-call of the world-all to awake —
We have seen and have heard,
Have perceived and breathed
The resonant hue, the awakening word
Of a Being of Sun —
Whose presence is the essence
Of the heaven's infinite gold,
Streamed-through and forever transmuted anew
By the healing, immaculate breath
Of burgeoning death;

Whose wonder and grace throughout all the ages
Cannot be told —
Spending a luminous, world-cleansing counsel
Clad in the boundless renewing of the deep inter-bueing
Of the meek with the bold —
A living, all-giving, all-caring One,
Who walks the earth
As the brother of men.

On the quest for the goal of man
Where the steadfast eyes of conscience,
Unwavering, warn and speak,

Light-loving souls of the laboring,
Who shall soon be a chorus of many —
Our forces ebbing, as we gaze aghast
Through the deepening doom of the world-storms' rage — —
There, out-beaming, fair, beyond compare,
On the vast, dark horizon of birth and of death,
We have glimpsed the first rays of the coming light-age,
Like the in-streaming shaft of a fresh life-breath
Of sun-drenched air,
And from heart's core declare to all in despair:

That by deed of that bounty which blooms
When the dawn of the spirit lightens and looms
At the lifting of the misting shadows of time,
Our conscious perceiving and inmost conceiving
Have been wakened and gifted to witness and see —
By the light of that sight, whereby the flood-fonts of truth
- In pure sun-tides of immediate being -
Route the clouds of all doubt:

No atom would be,
No land and no sea,
No streamlet could flow,
No seedling would grow,
No bud ever sprout —
Nor could insight illumine life's mystery,
Man's heart become free to love — without
The limitless boon of this Being of Sun,
Whose up-rising upholds
And whose whole love enfolds
Our planet earth,
Through all death and rebirth,
As the brother of men.

On the quest for the goal of man,
Where the loving gaze of conscience
Ever kindles courage and trust,

Light-welcoming souls of the waking,
Who shall once be the chorus of all,
In our uttermost plight we've been led by Your call,
Have been fed by Your sun, all-sharing One! —
Yet we carry the stain and endure the pain
Of the truth that all striving without You is vain;
The ache to be able to utter Your Name;
To have wisdom to serve the hush of Your flame!

For mankind is sick to the core for the sight of You,
Yet too weak to awake to the healing light of You —
To perceive, with heart-conscience, the selfless might of You! —

How there — alone, all-bearing — 'tis You
Who suffers for each and carries us through,
– Your mercy beneath us, Your promise above –
Till, fed by the fonts of Your life-source and love,
Through birth upon earth from life unto life,
We each shall remake and reshape our own way,
Each, for Your sake, shall purge his strife
In the truth where evil is burned away,
In the beauty that blooms from the bones of decay,
The goodness that glistens like dawn-lit dew
From the dark where death gives birth to the new;
Where the free awake to the voice of the day
And are able to say —
Not I but You, all-sharing One —
Yes, You in I — O Arisen Sun —
Dear brother of men!

VOICE

Of the Seeing and Remembering Heart

As when the sun
Beholds itself
In inmost glory,
And hears itself
As voice throughout the world —
'Tis so You stood before me,
Were
The instant quick
And very all of me —
The call,
Enfolding
The depths of hell
And all of heaven above
In one awakening Word,
One wound —
One living flood
Of unutterable
Love.

EASTER

The Voice of Awakening Man

Oh, do you know,
Are you aware,
That Christ is arisen
Everywhere!
That He moves and breathes
Through earth and air,
Enfolding each being in a bourne of light
That gifts the heart with a power of sight —
A sun-lit seeing
Of the essence of being —
As new and as fresh
As a frond in the spring,
As shy and swift
As a bird on the wing —
Revealing and awakening
Everything!

When your heart is aching,
Your whole soul shaking —
Can you not sense
The new dawn breaking! —

Under the clash and roar of steel
That rocks the nations and makes them reel,
Oh, can you not feel —
Like the cleansing core at the heart of a storm,
In the grace of His pure resurrected form,
How the cosmic springs of His life, His love and His being
Are cleansing the world — and feeding
The thirsting, arid wastes
Of the human race — freeing
The will-awakening tides
Of this heart-lit seeing
That hides
At the kernel of thought. . . .
That spaceless haven
Where love and freedom are breathed and wrought
And truth abides.

Oh, can you not see
With this dawning perceiving,
How His deed of healing —
Tender, outpouring,
Renewing, transforming —
Flows with a bounty that is quenchless, relentless,
With a freshening glory, defiled and defenseless
In the onslaughts of darkness —

Yet waking, shaking and shattering all
The empty machinations
Of Mammon's malignant mechanizations —
Till the towers of evil crumble and fall,
To lie like litter, aghast, in awful sprawl —
Transmuted to their foundations
To moldering loam for the seeds of life
By the chastening breath
Of His reticent might —

That matchless light
Of heaven's birth
On earth
Through death —
That moves and breathes
Through earth and air,
Enfolding each being
With loving care.

No single one need now despair —
For Christ is arisen
Every where!

WHITSUNTIDE

Choir-Call

Oh, awake!
  Awake — awake!
Let all cry out: Awake!
Each first unto himself and then for all to hear,
  Far and near —
Cry out: — Awaken, for God's sake!
  Before the human race goes down
  And our bewildered spirits drown
  In an ocean of mistake —
  Cry out, until our voices break —
  Awake! — Oh waken! —
  Till all mankind is shaken
  To the core
  And the mountains quake.

O sing!
  Sing — Come, sing!
All sing, sing out: Awake!
Across the breadths of space and time —
  Through all the gulfs of greed and grime,
  The blood-red tides of grief and crime,
  Until their turbid torrents ring!
Sing, sing, for pity's sake!
Until our urgent voices throb and sound
  Through every creature, heart and thing
  To bring to all
  This choir-call
  For our awakening!

Oh, speak!
  Speak — Yes, speak!
Let each speak out — for mercy's sake!
Before all human virtues disappear,
  Laid waste by impotence and fear.
Speak of this world-rending need — to wake!
Utter it, heart-lit and conscience-hewn,
  Each word, thought-chastened through and through,
  To him and her and you —

And self-heard — in that silent deep
Where each of us lies still asleep —
Until there be no longer one
Who does not hear — like shafts of sun —
This wonder-kindling word — Awake! —

And through the grace
That lights its all-illumining face,
  Its spirit-bidden power,
    Each hearing soul
Shall — waking! — see and know: —
    Yes! — 'Tis so! —

  In verity more true
Than all the breadths of cloudless blue —
    With You,
  O vast, awakening Word!
Who nowhere now cannot be heard —
Whose living human death,
Giving mankind spirit breath,
Is cosmic seed and birth
Of heaven's light and love on earth —
  The whole world too
    Is risen new!

And all this black impending storm
  Of infamy and wrong
  That shrouds us in death's keep,
  Robbed of respite or redress,
Is really wrought of naught but non-lit emptiness;
Is but the tragic, light-rejecting, self-condensing,
  Unawakened shadow only
  - Falling ever vainly dustward -
Of Your living, world-arisen form;

Is the dark, negating counter-image
Of that all-pervading, radiant presence
- Here upon our death-invaded earth -
    Of You,
  Who carry, with unwavering patience,
  All its hostile, un-lit harm
  In Your healing sun-lit calm!

  And the listening stars reply —
Their glistening language, heart-imperishably clear: —

Never more now need you fear!
Whatever evil may appear,
For you, yourself, at last now know
There is no darkness can deny:

The world is quick with burgeoning life and light,
A sheltering might,
Inviolately new! —
And is so, too, for you
When you awake!

And yet — until you do —
The life you sleep,
As falling shadow — doomed to die,
Is but a lie —

A captive of that counter-power
Who cannot give,
Cannot weep,
Cannot love, nor live,
Nor even die. . . .
But only take
And keep.

While life itself is risen whole
And true! —
Seed
And root,
Leaf and flower and fruit —
To feed

Man's famished, death-afflicted soul,
And nourish each
With sun-ability to reach
The loving, free immensity
Of his world-awaited goal.

So for man and earth and heaven's sake!
Whatever shadow fall — each day anew,
Thank the Risen Sun —
The loving One
Who wakens you!

MICHAELMAS

Voice of the Free Spirit of Man

O You
Who have given me
Your All
To be
My all
For me
And selflessly
Have set me free —

With all my heart,
My mind, my will.
Freely,
I take your gift —
Freely
Strive to be,
To become — to live
This new
World-mystery of me:

To do
Free deeds
Of courage and of love,
As pupil, artist, and as warrior
For the good, the beautiful, the true:
Conceived and wrought
With heaven-lit,
Heart-forged
Thought,
That cleaves with light
The shrouds below,
The sleep within,
The clouds above —

Till, suddenly,
Perceiving —
There amidst them all —
Your bleeding, earth-redeeming,
Free deed,

Your selfless healing
Of man's fall —
Stricken by its tender, vast, all-quickening
Wonder-call ...
Freeingly,
I answer
With my own
Awakening!

And answering —
Trembling there in the new air ...
Now armed at last with spears of sight
To pierce the dragon's brazen might;
Clothed with colors of compassion
To subdue the dazzling flocks of thirsting flight;
My thoughts star-sprung,
Like brimming well-springs bright,
I,
Who now have found myself to be
The wakening answer to your healing deed in me —

Freed,
As glad, light-gifted,
Life-up-lifted,
Sun-lit seeing,
Deep-will-rooted
Spirit being
- Minute morsel of world-man
Unfurled from slumber -

Freely now,
In flooding gratitude,
I give
This fresh-wrought fruit
Of all Your bounty,
This springing seed
Of Your free deed —
O great Giver of the All,
Dear All-Awakener! —
With all my heart
And meager art
To You.

CHRISTMAS — MIDWINTER

*Voices of the Wakeful
in Time of Darkness and Danger*

Christus sees in all dark,
Christus feels in each heart,
Christus heals in each harm,
Christus frees in all art.

—

CHORUS

For the Coming Age

New archangelic might
Is pouring from the heavens;

New Christ sight
Is awaking on the earth;

New human light
Is streaming
Through the gates of death and birth.

Out of cataclysmic strife,
The new mysteries of life —
The new light age
Of the Risen One
Has at last begun —

Its myriad redeeming deeds
Flocking to be done;
Its apocalyptic victories —
Wide-winged — waiting to be won! . . .

Through every dark, its mercy-call
Summons now the hearts of all;

Its living-fingered light unbinds
The frozen shrouds that blind men's minds,
Sets free each will — that everyone
May join the warriors of the sun,
In rescue of that spirit core
That all the universe is for.

—

YELLOW ROSEBUSH BY THE DOOR

Dear yellow rosebush by the door,
Mounting heavenward with a store,
A radiant throng,
Of softly-scented golden blooms
In clambering song —
A sun-filled galaxy of grace
In glad release
Of such outpouring, rhythmic peace
As no mortal thought can match,
Nor doubt destroy —
Spraying wide in arched festoons
Of June-bright joy.

Only so soon — too soon! — to fall —
Scattering their all
In showers of petaled rain
To deck the earth's glad, upturned face
With a parable of bridal lace,
In fulfillment of the sun-lit lore
Of the holy sacrament
Once more.

Ah, yellow rosebush by the door —
In face of every woe and wrong,
Again and ever yet again
Within my heart
May I adore,
Like you,
The Sun —
The Risen One —
With such pure-petaled song,
Forever more.

CHILD'S PRAYER

The golden sun so great and bright
Warms the world with all its might.
It makes the dark earth green and fair,
And tends each thing with ceaseless care.
It shines on blossom, stone and tree,
On bird and beast, on you and me.
Oh, may each deed throughout the day,
May everything I do and say,
     Be bright and good and true —
     O golden sun — like you!

—

The gentle meadows are still sweet with new mown hay,
Soft bird songs echo through the wood and one by one,
Like clear drops, cease — till all is still. The world takes breath,
And all creation quivers as the day is done.

While there above the mountains, see! in bleeding silence
The sun has poured his whole heart's blood across the sky,
As if in infinite compassion and mute grief
For all the wrong and infamy of those who die.

A deeply moving, ever-changing, weaving, gleaming —
As if angelic hosts were gathering to choir
Their glowing harmonies through all the breadths of heaven,
The bright drops flow and bathe the earth in cleansing fire.

O mighty, bleeding heart who breaks for love of man —
I reach out all my being like an empty bowl
To catch the tender, healing, holy crimson streaming
Of Your outpouring life and will. — Oh, fill me whole!

What right have I,
With all my erring ways and faults,
The doubts and vanities that rise
Still untransformed in me,
To sing of You,
O Blesser of the blest,
In cosmic magnitudes of virtue
The most high! —
And yet, before I die,
And leave for some yet hidden time
This wonder-woven, wound-torn earth,
Which You have hallowed as Your home,
I cannot rest,
Unless I try! —

Perhaps I only desecrate,
With all too many words
And fumbling praise,
Your faultless grace —
And, seeking to reveal,
But veil Your face.

And yet, with all my lack and littleness,
Have I the right,
In this dark plight
Of man's forgetfulness of You,
To quail,
To fail
To speak my heart,
That owes to You its light —
To speak my mind,
That knows through You the true —
With words,
Whose wonder Your high hosts have wrought
As vessels for Your all-conceiving thought —
Fail, to use their brimming gifts
To utter, humbly, who it is
To whom our very life and all
Are due —

And, doubting Your divine forgiveness
Of our all-recurring fall,
Through fear of my own ill,
Remain mute and still? —

So may the love that wells,
The thanks that grows and flows,
The trickling stream of heaven's poesie
That gleams and swells
In me,
Through Your unfailing art,
The free resolve, long ripened in my heart,
Outweigh, I pray,
Transmute,
In ever worthier degree,
Within my words,
Their malady.

—

When a word that we have wrought
Flowers in another's thought,
When it ripens to a seed
As another's living deed —
Then an angel picks it up,
Places it in heaven's cup,
Smiles, that such sweet grain has grown,
Keeps it till it may be sown —
And from such kernels makes the bread
With which — all mankind is fed.

For K. v. O.

There is a golden merriment
No evil can destroy
Or ever touch,
No shadow scar,
Because its quality is such
As no impurity can mar.

There is a joy,
Of such unburdening degree,
No enmity can ever grow
Within its glow —
So free
That it can dwell
And spend its fervency,
Its loving, high festivity,
As well
In heaven as in hell.

There is a beauty,
That turns all labor
And all duty
Into love,
And brings to earth the flavor
Of the starry meadow-land
Above.

And there is then a trust,
No matter what we must,
That flows
Into the soul
From each undeviable star,
That knows
Itself at one
With that vast, sparkling whole,
Its innermost confiding goal,
That is the cure
For every human ill —
And will
Throughout eternity,
In pure,
Infallible security,
Endure.

Befriended and attended by
Such merriment and beauty,
Untrammeled joy and trust,
Man, as spirit being,
Incarnate in earth-dust,
Can again, and ever yet again,
Fulfill, at will,
A tiny free
Unfolding grain
Of his own
High, star-sown
Identity.

Love's selfless demonstration
That truth —
While gazing with the cloudless lense
Of celestial sight
Into the springs of its own
Infallible creation —
Floods all the perishable world
With the quenchless might
Of imperishable youth.

—

THEY WAIT!

Walk lovingly and firmly on the earth.
You tread the living substance of rebirth.

Drink deep the water from the welling spring.
Its life-font now baptizes everything.

Breathe gratefully the selfless, viewless air
That spreads the spirit's message everywhere.

And talk with hallowed heart-beat with the sun
Who speaks the language of the Risen One.

They wait, all four, for you, man, now to wake! —
And share the single source of all their worth,

That they may heal, and not, through *you*, destroy
The bounty of this death-endangered earth.

With every outstretched hand we clasp,
Of stranger, loved-one, friend or foe,
Wherever we may be, or go!
It is Your flesh our fingers grasp,
Your Being whom we learn to know.

Yes, every daily human meeting
With those who tread this sore-tried earth,
Brings to us a loving greeting
Of unfathomable worth.

For You are hidden in each mortal,
Who is for us a star-wrought portal
To find in You our spirit birth,
In each, the healing of all dearth.

—

Creative spirits, in self-conquest,
Beam like beacons in the night —
Human light-houses unshaken
Amidst the tempests of man's plight.

Though scattered far and few — engulfed
In wastes of evil, bleak, obscure —
They shine like stars out of the gloom,
A gleaming heaven in miniature.

For in themselves they wage the war
Which others vent with outward force,
Till, breaking wide the siege of darkness,
They free the sun-power at their source.

From the womb of crumbling chaos
They toil to give it form and birth —
Cause the wonder of the firmament
To bloom upon the blighted earth.

As singers in orchestral choir,
Each rejoices in his heart
To share in glad companionship
The love of labor in such art.

So, though mankind be steeped in ruin,
His pomp a morass of decline,
Yet from this dire disintegration
Human stars — free spirits — shine!

Oh, take courage! Courage!
And then take courage once again!
All the evil is but there
To whet your blunted blade of sight
To see
Life's overarching artistry. —
Its vast, awe-inwrought harmony
Of sacrificial mastery!

All the turmoil, crime and pain,
Subterfuge and savagery,
The pride and greed dire hosts disgorge,
Are loosed again and yet again
To fan the fires of your will
To dare —
Dare to look upon man's shame!
Sieze your seeing's clean, sharp flame
And in its pure sun-molten light,
- Piercing hell and star-thronged height -
Dare, with all your heart, to forge,
From the raw, unhallowed ore,
The humble goblet of the good,
The vehicle of brotherhood —
That fragile vessel which alone can hold,
Receive and then outpour,
The liquid gold
Of love's unerring remedy —
Earth's sun-sweet, purging mystery —
The nectar of the free.

Oh, take courage! Courage!
And then take courage thrice again!
Through evil's onslaughts
See! —
With pure sun-thoughts
Look each demon in the eye,
Redeeming there its hidden lie.
And with your whole heart's blood,
All its loving, light-transmuted, ever-flowing flood,
Dare,
With your Angel's helping care,
To share
In the healing alchemy
Of human-cosmic destiny.

Only the giver
Is given —
Only the hollow bowl,
Offering its whole,
Can be filled
To overflowing —

Only the proffered soul,
Cleansed,
Through its own free control,
Of its clamour and strife,
Hold
The liquid of knowing —

The eternal flowing
Of love
In the glistening stream
Of the waters of life.

—

Postlude

LIFE-WAY TO THE SPIRIT

How can we see
With the eye
Of a seeing so free,
Yet so sunlit,
We can see in the seen
The Spirit within it?

How can we hear
With the ear
Of a hearing so clear,
Yet so lowly,
We can hear in the heard
The Spirit that is Holy?

How can we speak
With the voice
Of a speaking so meek,
Yet so world-knit,
We can speak the speech
Of the Holy Spirit?

When thinking becomes seeing,
When feeling has won hearing,
When willing has begun speaking
The lore of love's teaching —
Then the Holy Spirit will come
And lead us to the One
We are seeking.

—

INDEX

First Lines and Titles